Holiday Parties for Children

Holiday Parties for Children

A Complete Planning Guide

by

ANITA M. SMITH

McFarland & Company, Inc., Publishers
Jefferson, North Carolina, and London

Library of Congress Cataloguing-in-Publication Data

Smith, Anita M.
    Holiday parties for children : a complete planning
guide / by Anita M. Smith.
        p.   cm.
    Includes index.
    ISBN 0-7864-0802-2 (softcover : 50# alkaline paper) ∞
    1. Children's parties — Planning.   2. Holidays.   I. Title.
GV1205.S54   2000
793.2'1 — dc21   00-44218

British Library cataloguing data are available

Cover image ©2000 Artville

Manufactured in the United States of America

*McFarland & Company, Inc., Publishers
    Box 611, Jefferson, North Carolina 28640
    www.mcfarlandpub.com*

For my children, Tony and Nicole — my inspiration.
And to my mother, Louise,
who started it all, and always taught me
to be a creative thinker. Love ya!

Acknowledgments

For their input, inspiration and constant encouragement during all the years that I have worked on this book, I extend my love and deepest thanks...

To my husband, Hugh Smith,

To my children, Tony and Nicole Smith,

To my parents, John and Louise DeRosia,

To my sisters, Debbie Wheeler, Linda DeCiantis, and Lisa Montgomery,

To my grandparents, Yelma Marini and the late Ernest Marini,

To all of the homeroom parents, PTO members and teachers at Union United Methodist Church Preschool, H.E. Corley Elementary, Dutch Fork Elementary, River Springs Elementary, and CrossRoads Middle schools in Irmo, S.C.,

To my former teaching colleagues of children's religious education at Our Lady of the Hills Catholic Church in Columbia, S.C.,

To all of the volunteers and employees at the Richland Co. Public Library for planning some of the best children's events ever,

And to my many friends and neighbors in Irmo, S.C., who have given me some fantastic material and have helped in the testing of many of these parties.

I would also like to thank Karen Dively, Lori Hammond, Mary Anne Coumo, and Jamie Barrett for their contributions.

Anita M. Smith

Table of Contents

Introduction

Chances are, planning holiday parties will be a part of your life at some time or another. Often times we are asked by our children's teachers to plan parties or events that we just aren't sure we can handle. Or perhaps your neighborhood association or church has decided to put you in charge of planning this year's holiday event. No matter what the circumstances, even the most experienced party planner can feel a little overwhelmed when asked to be in charge of putting an event together. Sometimes we just need to hear tips or suggestions from others who have been there. Successful event or party planners are those who are open to new ideas. This book was put together for those of you who are searching for some great new ideas and tips.

The holidays that I have included are the most common holidays celebrated in the United States. This book is arranged by holiday dates that are spread throughout the year so that you will always be prepared.

Many of the chapters have more ideas than you may be able to use, so that you can pick and choose new ideas each year. You could even flip through all of the chapters when preparing for a certain holiday to find ideas that can be adapted to the holiday theme that you are using.

Smile, have fun, and happy holidays!

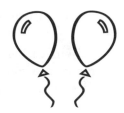

Planning Your Event or Party

🎉 ENLIST 🎉 A HELPER

Planning an event or party with one or more helpers not only lessens the workload for you, but it makes the process more enjoyable. If you are a room parent for your child's class, get one or more assistants to help you out throughout the school year. Try to get another parent that you know well or enjoy being with. If you aren't familiar with any of the parents yet, then try to get a parent of your child's good friend. You will have something in common, and when you get together to plan for the parties or events your children can play with one another.

If the event that you are planning is for your neighborhood, then ask a good neighbor to help you out. You could even ask other neighbors from each end of the neighborhood to help. If you gather helpers from all over the neighborhood, then they can introduce you to people that you may not know, bringing the entire neighborhood closer together — which is the whole meaning behind having neighborhood or block parties.

If you are planning a family reunion or gathering, give everyone a list of something to bring or something to do. The more involved the merrier. If grandma makes the best apple pie anyone has ever tasted, and she would be honored to make it, then that could be all that she needs to bring. If someone isn't well or just hates to cook, then give them something simple to bring such as paper goods. Suppose you have a relative who is struggling financially but insists on bringing something. Ask that person to bring something that doesn't cost anything, such as tables and chairs that he or she already owns. You could also ask for that person's

3

help in setting up at the party or helping you to cook. You get the picture: Fit the need to the helper.

☙ HOLD A ☙ MEETING

With schedules as hectic as they are for many, getting together with your assistants to plan your event or party may seem impossible. If all you have time for is a phone call, then that will have to do. Your meeting may be limited time-wise, so try to get the planning done first. Once the schedule or shopping list has been made, then you will feel free to talk about other things.

Getting together with your helpers to plan is necessary and should be done well in advance. You may need to reserve a building, a park area, or equipment for your party or event. Many times these get booked months before they are needed. This is especially true of carnival equipment in the springtime, when many churches, schools and cities have carnivals and festivals. So, if you want to get the spot or item before someone else does, call as soon as you have set a date with your assistant.

Another reason you will want to plan well in advance is to let a teacher know of your plans. That way, he will be able to prepare for your arrival. When planning for a neighborhood event, remember that neighbors like to plan any vacations around the events. If your neighborhood or church has a bulletin or newsletter, let everyone know about the upcoming event by using this means of communication well in advance.

Before you meet with your assistant, go through the book and choose the crafts, games, activities, etc., which you are interested in. When you meet, discuss them and decide if they are appropriate for the age and number of your group. Most likely, you will like things that your assistant won't — even if you are the best of friends. That is fine. Within reason, go with the flow. You will need to get along with this person, and you depend on her help to make everything work, so compromise.

Once I had an assistant who insisted that nine year olds were too old for crafts. I absolutely disagreed. So we compromised and did half as many crafts as I would have liked to. We instead planned other activities, which went over great. But to my assistant's surprise, the children also loved the crafts. All in all, the children had so much fun that they asked us if we could be their homeroom moms for the next year. So I think that we were both right, and I am glad that we listened to one another.

As strange as it may seem, some assistants may feel put out if you don't allow them to do half of all buying, baking and planning. If your assistant is this type, by all means give that person half of all of the responsibility, and be thankful that he is so willing to help you.

A day or two before the party or event, call your assistant to make sure he will be there when expected and has done all that he or she agreed to do.

🎉 BUDGET 🎉 OR FUNDING

If there is a special fund set up for the party or event, this can help out tremendously, but it can also be quite a headache. No matter how you pay for your party or event, you may need to keep within a certain spending limit. Sometimes the dollar amounts that you are given can fall quite short of what is needed to plan the party or event.

In such cases, you will need to ask volunteers to help supply needed food or materials. Don't try to pay for everything out of your own pocket unless you are planning a personal party at your home (for example a birthday party). You would be surprised at how willing others will be to help you — as long as you don't ask too often.

Ask different people for help for different parties or events, so that they don't feel as if they are the only ones helping out. And you won't feel as if you are overburdening anyone. Also, the cost will be evenly distributed among all of the parents or guests, not just a select few.

Send potential helpers a note through their children or call them at home to ask them for assistance. If you are very pleasant and polite with them, they are most likely going to be willing to help out.

🎉 INVITATIONS 🎉

One of the great things about having a class party at a school is that there is no need for sending out invitations. You already know that almost everyone will be there. But holding an event or party under any other circumstance requires plenty of promotion to make it work.

Large-scale school, church, neighborhood, or community events can be advertised with flyers passed out to everyone. You can use the wording in the examples shown in each chapter. If possible, use a computer to print up fliers with a professional look. If you need to print a lot of copies and don't have a large copier available, take your fliers to a copy center to have copies made.

For a small family or neighborhood gathering, just make your invitations as shown in each chapter.

Your invitation or flyer should state the type of event or party that you will be having, the date, a rain date (for outdoor parties and events), time, place, and name and phone number of someone who can be contacted with questions or responses.

🎉 HIRING 🎉 ENTERTAINMENT

Before hiring any entertainment, check out references. If possible, go watch the entertainer in action. Make sure that the entertainer is exciting to watch and can hold the audience's attention. When planning a carnival or festival, check with national restaurant and grocery store chains to see if they have costumed characters they could send out to the event. Many of them will send their employees out for free as an advertising gimmick for their business. Some will pass out trinkets or coloring books. Also check with your local forestry commission to see if they can send out a costumed Smokey the Bear.

🎉 DECORATIONS 🎉

Decorations shouldn't be necessary if you are holding the party in a classroom or church. Most likely, these settings will already have some decorations.

If the party is to be held at your home, you may already have some holiday decorations in place. See each chapter for some great decorating suggestions.

When holding the party or event at a rented building or park, a little decorating may be necessary. In a park you can often use fences or poles to hang your decorations from. Just be sure to remove them when you leave.

🎉 ARRIVAL 🎉 OF GUESTS

As guests arrive, let them know where to put any belongings and offer them something to eat or drink. With a class party, obviously all of the children know one another, but your assistants may have never met before. Introduce those who don't know one another. Introduce new neighbors at block parties.

At community events, just be friendly and welcome everyone. At a family reunion, most everyone will know one another, but introduce those who are new to the family (e.g., new spouses, boyfriends, girlfriends, relatives from out of state, etc.).

Once everyone has arrived, begin with the crafts, games and activities that you have planned.

🎉 SETTING 🎉 UP AREAS

Over the years, I have noticed that planning a party or event for a large group is very, very different from planning a small group party. Chances are that it will be too difficult to handle a large group of children if they are all working on one craft or game at once. Setting up different areas to disperse the group really helps keep things under control.

Assign one or two adults or teens to be at each area. For example, if you have two crafts and two games planned, have two different craft tables set up with the necessary craft supplies on them and one or two parents seated at each table. Place the games on the other side of the room or area with one or two adults in charge of running each.

Try to choose wisely when deciding which person will run each area. Obviously, putting a person with little or no patience at an area that requires a lot of patience is going to ruin the craft or game for the children participating in it. So ask the assistants where they feel most comfortable helping out, or use your best judgment.

🎉 CRAFTS 🎉

Purchase or save any needed crafts materials well in advance. This is especially true around the Christmas season. Many people make craft items during the holidays, and you may have trouble finding the items that you need if you wait too long. Also, enlist your assistants' or relatives' help in saving any recyclable items needed for crafts. Save scrap materials from household decorating or sewing projects.

Always make a sample of each craft to be made at the party or event. This is done for two reasons: First, you need to know exactly how the craft is made so that you can show your guests how to make it. Second, if the children can see the finished product, then it will be easier for them to understand how the craft should look as they are making it.

If you are planning a messy craft project, ask your guests to come dressed in old playclothes so that they do not ruin their good clothes. Have the children roll up their sleeves to help keep them clean.

For small-scale parties, make the crafts at the beginning of the party to allow time for drying. It is also nice to begin a party with a calm activity such as a craft. For a large-scale event, the children will be making their crafts at different times.

🎉 GAMES AND 🎉 ACTIVITIES

For the children (and many of us older folks), playing games is probably the most important and memorable thing about a party or event. Hey, who doesn't like to have a good time? A party just isn't any fun without games!

Try out the games before the day of the party or event to give you an idea of how they work and how long each will take. How many games you plan will depend on how many guests will be playing them, how much time you have, the age and ability of the guests and the area that you will be playing the games in.

Plan for a few more games than you think you will need. These should be games that do not require any construction or added expense, just in case you do not use them. Use these games if you have extra time and need to keep your guests busy. Many games listed for certain parties can be played more than once, if the need should arise. Many times a certain game will be such a hit that your guests will want to play it over and over.

Try to have a good mix of active and quiet games. Always try to play quiet games after everyone has eaten to allow everyone's food time to settle. This is especially true on hot summer days. For outdoor parties, plan some games that can be played indoors in case it should rain and things need to be moved indoors.

When choosing teams for games, try to make sure that each team has players equal in size and ability. That way one team will not have an advantage over another. Adults can fill in when a team has one less player than another.

Move quickly from one activity to the next to discourage talk of winners or losers. That way no one ever gets a chance to brood on the subject. Everyone will be too busy having fun to care about such matters.

Many children 5 and under do not like blindfolds and can become frightened by them, so allow them to cover their eyes or just close them if they like.

To clearly mark game boundaries, start lines, finish lines, throw lines or goals, use things like sport field cones, garden hoses, fences, yard sticks, door mats, masking tape, chalk, paper plates, string, or chairs. Just choose the item that fits the type of game best. Always keep safety in mind and never use an item that can injure a person should he fall on it. For example, you would not want to use rocks, wires, or stakes as a goal in a game, especially a running game. Running games should always have a marker that is securely in place, but not anything the runner could trip over.

🎉 PRIZES 🎉

At many carnivals and events prizes are expected, but for a neighborhood gathering or family gathering they are usually not. For a small party at your house, the choice is yours. If your party has children 5 and under, then you may choose to award everyone a prize after a game, or you may not want to award any at all. Children of this young age really do not understand the concept of winning and losing, and shouldn't be expected to. Older children, on the other hand, are getting a better grasp on the concept and may expect a prize.

If your budget doesn't allow giving prizes then don't give them. But if you like, give small prizes such as a piece of candy. If you should decide to award prizes for games, make sure that everyone wins one before it is time to go home. You can make up a reason to give them one, such as for being the "best helper," "most patient," "most polite," etc.

🎉 GOODY BAGS 🎉 AND PARTY FAVORS

For large-scale events goody bags are not expected. At some schools, churches and small parties they may be expected. What you put in a goody bag—if you use them at all—depends on what you feel comfortable with. If all that you want to put in the bags is a small amount of candy, then that is fine. Each chapter lists many more party theme related favor and prize ideas than you could ever possibly use. This is done to give you a variety of ideas to choose from.

Wait until the end of the party to pass out the goody bags to prevent mix-ups. Since mix-ups will still occur, label each child's goody bag with his or her name.

Many things can be used as a goody or favor holder. You can use holiday themed buckets or bags, decorated paper bags, zippered sandwich bags, tissue paper tied with ribbon, beach pails, etc.

Many cities have party supply stores where you can purchase holiday themed party favors. But if you have trouble finding such a store, the following are two of my favorite mail order companies that sell party supplies:

Oriental Trading Co., Inc.
P.O. Box 3407
Omaha, NE 68103-0407
1-800-228-2269
Website: *http://www.oriental.com*

U.S. Toy
1227 E. 119th St.
Grandview, MO 64030-1117
1-800-255-6124
(in Kansas City area call 816-761-5900)

☃ PARTY ☃ PRECAUTIONS

Most likely, the following precautions are ones that you have already practiced around your home for years. I will mention them anyway, just in case.

- Before guests arrive, put pets away in a safe place. This is both to protect them and to protect your guests. Make sure that your pet is comfortable and well fed.

- Keep all flammable items, such as party decorations, away from heat sources.

- Keep bandages and peroxide on hand for any little cuts that may occur.

- Learn some basic CPR. Chances are that you won't need it, but it is always good to know.

- Go through your yard or the party area before the day of the party or event and check for any potential hazards. Check fences and decks for popped nails or sharp points, clear the yard of debris, and put hammocks away.

- Never leave uninflated balloons where small children or pets can get them. They can easily choke on them. Do not take metallic balloons outdoors near power lines. If they come in contact with power lines they can cause serious problems.

- Choose party favors wisely for young children. Favors for children under 3 should not be smaller than 1¼-inch.

- Never leave handguns, fireworks, medication or chemicals where children can get them. Keep them in a locked cabinet.

- Do not leave children unattended, especially near water.

☃ THANK ☃ YOUR ASSISTANTS

All of us like to know that the efforts we have given to a party or event have been appreciated. Personally thank all of your helpers for the things that they have done to make the day a success, and thank them for coming. If someone has baked an incredible eye-catching batch of cupcakes, be sure to mention how impressed you are. Or, if the game that your assistant came up with was a smashing hit, let her know.

A day or two after the party or event is over, send your assistants a thank you note telling them that you couldn't have pulled it off without their help. Thank them for any donations that they gave and for help with any games or crafts that they were in charge of.

If sending thank you notes would be too daunting because the event had a very large number of volunteers, then make sure that you at least write a gen-eral thank you to everyone who helped out. Publish it in a newsletter that will already be distributed to those in-volved. People are sure to appreciate your mentioning and acknowledging their efforts and will probably look for-ward to helping you in the future.

One person who is sure to be grateful for your efforts in putting to-gether such a great party or event is your child. It is certainly worth the effort that is put into it. It is my most sincere hope that this book will bring together family, friends, neighbors, teachers and children for happy, mem-orable good times.

I wish you very happy holiday cel-ebrations!

New Year's Eve Party

• *December 31* •

Would you like to ring in the New Year with a big bang? Why not consider a New Year's Eve Party that both children and adults can enjoy? Some parents may be glad that they will have someone to watch their child, so that they can go out. Others may like to spend New Year's with their child, so it may be a good idea to check with family and friends before planning this party. This party would be a great get together for your family, close friends and their children. Some people have New Year's Eve parties and just let the children invited stay the night and the parents go home after the party. If your guests must leave before midnight, or don't want to keep their children up until midnight, celebrate the New Year at 9:00 P.M. or 10:00 P.M. If you like, make this a costume party and ask your guests to come dressed in any costume that they desire. However you

plan to celebrate, your party is sure to be a fun way to ring in the New Year with the many ideas in this chapter!

☝ CLOCK ☝ INVITATION

You will need:

White posterboard

Scissors

Black construction paper

Fasteners (found in office supply stores or department stores), 1 per invitation

Markers

What to do:

1. Trace circles about 4 inches in

diameter on the posterboard, using a cup or bowl to trace around. If you will be hand delivering your invitations you can make the circles larger. Cut out the circles.

2. Write the numbers 1–12 on the circle just as a clock face would appear.

3. Make clock hands out of construction paper and attach them to the face of the clock with a paper fastener.

4. Write the party details on the back of the invitation as illustrated (fig. 1a & b).

♟ DECORATIONS ♟

• Put a sign on the front door that reads "HAPPY NEW YEAR!" Many party supply stores have great New Year's Eve decorations. If the weather is warm where you live, attach some balloons to the sign.

• Hang a banner from a dining room doorway or fireplace mantle (if you won't be lighting a fire in the fireplace) that reads "HAPPY NEW YEAR!" Tie balloons to the corners of the doorway or mantle.

• Hang balloons and curled ribbon from light fixtures (keeping away from the heat source).

• Make clocks and hourglasses out of construction paper and hang in the party room.

• Decorate the table with a colorful tablecloth, and throw confetti and curled ribbon on it. You can even use New Year's Eve decorated tableware.

• Put one or more cordless clocks in the center of the table. Set them to go off at the stroke of midnight, or whatever time you have chosen to celebrate the New Year.

• Supply horns, noisemakers or even

(a)

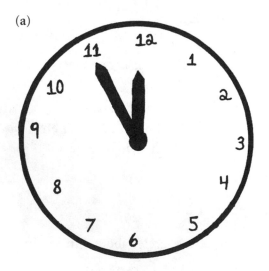

(b)

Fig. 1. Clock Invitation

pots and pans for guests to bang and make plenty of noise at midnight, or the hour that you will be celebrating the New Year.

- Play songs like "Auld Lang Syne," "(We're Gonna) Rock Around the Clock" (Bill Haley and His Comets) "Calendar Girl" (Neil Sedaka) or "January, February, March..." (Marcy Marxer).

🎉 FOOD 🎉

In Spain and many Latin American countries, it is a custom to eat twelve grapes or twelve raisins for luck at the twelve strokes of midnight. Each stroke stands for one of the twelve months of the year. In Mexico it is customary to drink steaming mugs of hot chocolate for luck on New Year's Eve. In the southern region of the United States many people eat black-eyed peas for good luck on New Year's Eve. If you live in a region that is cold on New Year's Eve, serve warm foods such as the following:

- Jambalaya or chili
- Crunchy French bread or cheese and crackers
- Grapes, twelve per guest
- Clock Cookies: sugar cookies with 12 dots and clocks hands piped on
- Ginger ale, sparkling grape juice, warm spiced cider or hot chocolate

Clock Cake

You will need:

1 two layer 8- or 9-inch baked cake
4 cups white frosting
Any color food coloring you choose for the clock face

What to do:

1. Bake and cool the cake as directed. Frost the entire cake white.

2. Color the remaining frosting. Pipe a shell border around the top and bottom edge of the cake, using a frosting bag fit with a star tip.

3. Switch to a small round tip and pipe on numbers just as a clock face looks. Frost on the hands to point at twelve midnight.

🎉 ARRIVAL 🎉 OF GUESTS

As each guest arrives, plant a goofy New Year's Eve hat on his head.

🎉 CRAFTS 🎉

Foam Snowmen

You will need:

Foam balls, 2 per guest
Toothpicks, 2–3 per guest
Brown pipe cleaners, 2 per guest

Construction paper: orange, black, brown, etc.

Glue

Cloth material, optional

What to do:

1. Lay all of the supplies out on a table, which has been covered with a paper tablecloth or newspaper.
2. Connect the 2 foam balls with one or more toothpicks in the center, forming a head and a body.
3. Decorate the balls, using pipe cleaners for the stick arms, and the construction paper for the eyes, nose, mouth, buttons, etc. Cut a strip of cloth to make a scarf and fringe it. Wrap it around the neck of the snowman and glue it in place.

Finger Puppets

Now here is a craft to help you get rid of all of those annoying pairs of odd gloves hanging around your house. If your house is anything like mine, you have at least 5 pairs of cleaning gloves for the hand that you never use, because you have worn out all of the ones for the hand that you *do* use. Or maybe your children somehow mysteriously have a habit of losing their gloves, leaving you with a glove with no match. Well, if you just can't bear to throw the odd gloves away, use them for this craft!

You will need:

Old gloves

Decorations: fabric scraps, cotton balls, tiny pompoms, wiggle eyes, pipe cleaners, etc.

Glue

Scissors

Felt tip markers

What to do:

1. Before the party, cut all of the fingers off of the gloves, leaving you with the body of the character to be created. Discard the remaining part of the glove.
2. During the party, lay all of the supplies out on a table, which has been covered with a paper tablecloth or newspaper. Let the children cut out little hats from the fabric. Use the pompoms for the tops of the hats, or use them as noses. Use cotton for hair, beards or fur. Create anything that comes to mind.

New Year's Eve Noisemakers

See Cinco de Mayo Festival/Mexican Fiesta Craft, Maracas.

🎉 GAMES AND 🎉 ACTIVITIES

Resolutions

You will need:

Sheets of paper, 1 per guest

Pencils, 1 per guest

A bowl or hat

What to do:

1. Each guest writes down a New Year's resolution for himself, but does not sign his name to it.

2. An adult walks around and collects the resolutions in a bowl or a hat, and then he mixes them up.

3. He then reads them to all of the guests, one at a time. The rest of the guests must try to guess who has written the resolution. If no one can guess, the person who wrote the resolution must confess.

Artists' Beat the Clock

You will need:

2 large pads of drawing paper
2 easels, optional
2 felt tip markers
A timer
Cards with words of things to draw: a truck, a computer, a baseball, a steaming teapot, a cat, money, etc.

What to do:

1. Divide guests into two equal teams. Choose one guest from each team to come up and look at one of the cards. Don't let the other guests see the cards. The first two players who have read the card must try to draw the picture that describes the word.

2. Once the timer is set, the players may begin to draw. Set the timer for 1 minute. They can draw as much as they want in that 1 minute to try to get their team members to guess the word. They hold the pad so that the other team members can see the pad, if you do not have two easels for them to place the pads on.

3. The first team to guess the word correctly scores a point. Then another two team members come up and do as the first two team members have. The game continues, until all of the cards have been used. The team with the most points wins.

The Year's Top 10

This game may be best suited for adults or older children, such as teenagers, since some younger children may not be as familiar with world events. Hand each guest a piece of a paper and a pencil. Ask them to write 10 of the most memorable or important things that have happened during the past year. Save a newspaper or magazine that may have all of the most important events listed. Keep them as a reference for yourself, but don't allow anyone else to see it. Some events might be the new fame or death of an important person, the release of the best selling movie of all time, a natural disaster, the election of a new president, the beginning or ending of a war, the latest space exploration, etc. Anyone who can come up with 10 actual important events listed in your newspaper or magazine wins a prize.

Balloon Surprises

You will need:

Balloons, 1 per guest

Small trinkets, 1 per guest: erasers, rings, plastic figures, etc.

A pin

What to do:

1. Before the party, place one trinket into each balloon. Inflate the balloon and tie it closed.

2. After the stroke of "midnight" go around with a pin and pop each guest's balloon for them. They get to keep the surprise.

Caution: Immediately throw away any broken balloon pieces to prevent small children and pets from choking on them.

Balloon Fortunes

Do the same as with the activity Balloon Surprises, but instead of putting a trinket in the balloon, put a written paper fortune inside of the balloon. See the following examples:

For parties with elementary and middle school aged children write:

"You will get a new bike within the next year."

"You will get all A's on your report card for the next year."

"You will have the best birthday of your life this year."

"The boy/girl that you like will like you too."

"The next year will be the happiest year of your life."

"You will get a lot of homework in school this year."

"You will be getting a raise in your allowance this year."

For parties with teenagers or adults write:

"You will be getting a nice car this year."

"You will be getting a new job this year."

"You will meet a great new boyfriend/girlfriend this year." (For teens and singles.)

"You will be getting a raise at your current job this year."

"You will get a good income tax refund this year."

"You will win a nice prize soon."

"The New Year will be a happy one for you."

Lucky Month

You will need:

Pieces of paper with one month of the year written on each piece

Masking tape

Music to play such as "Calendar Girl" (Neil Sedaka)

What to do:

1. Tape the months on the floor or ground, in a circle, with the masking tape. Have each guest stand on a month. If there are more than 12 guests, have them double up, two to a month, or make some papers blank.

2. An adult writes a month on a piece of paper, but conceals the month.

3. As the music begins playing, all of the players begin walking around the circle clockwise.

4. When the music stops, anyone standing on the month written down before the music started wins a prize. An appropriate prize would be a calendar for

the coming year. You may want to have a few calendars available, so that you can play a few rounds of this game.

Rock Around the Clock

Play this game just as you would the game Lucky Month as described above, but instead of writing a name of a month on each sheet of paper write the numbers 1–12 on them. Play the game to the song "(We're Gonna) Rock Around the Clock" (Bill Haley and His Comets). With this version of the game anyone caught standing on the number 12 (or the stroke of midnight) is the winner. An appropriate prize would be a clock cake or clock cookies for parties with older guests, or posters of rock groups for parties with younger guests.

Sing at the Stroke of Midnight

In the English-speaking countries of the Americas, it is customary to sing "Auld Lang Syne" on New Year's Eve. The words are sung in Scottish dialect. They mean "old long since," or "days gone by." Check your local library, music store or department store for a tape of Christmas holiday songs that may contain this song. You may even want to check in holiday songbooks for this song. Copy the words on individual songsheets, so that everyone may join in to sing the song at "midnight." If you actually let the children stay up

until midnight, many television stations play the song at midnight.

Balloon Drop

Inflate a large quantity of balloons and place them in a net or a large basket. Write the number 12 on one of the balloons. Drop the balloons over the guests just after the stroke of "midnight." If possible, drop the balloons from a high place such as a stairway banister. The guest to find the number 12 balloon wins a prize.

Variation: If you decide not to use a large quantity of balloons, you could just drop one weighted balloon from the ceiling or stairway as a way of signaling that the New Year has arrived.

FAVOR AND PRIZE IDEAS

Just before it is time for the children to go home, have an adult sneak a bag of goodies into each child's shoes. Tell the children that Father Time has filled them. Some good favor and prize ideas are: New Year's party hats, noisemakers, horns, whistles, pocket-sized calendars for the coming year, horoscope books, diaries, hourglass-shaped egg timers filled with sand, Foam Snowmen (see Crafts), Finger Puppets (see Crafts), trinkets for Balloon Surprises (see Activity), or clock cookies (see Food).

Chinese New Year Party

• *Between January 21* •
and February 19

Now here's a party you and your child will go gung-ho over! In China and other parts of the Far East, the celebration of the Chinese New Year is also a giant birthday party. Most everyone in China celebrates the coming of the New Year as a birthday party for all. Everyone, including babies, is considered one year older during the celebration. "Happy New Year" is the theme of the spring festival celebrations that marks the lunar New Year in China. Records of the festival date back more than 2,000 years. The New Year is a time of noisemaking, wearing new clothes, exchanging presents, feasting and visiting family and friends. Adults stay up late to scare away evil spirits. The Chinese New Year is a four-day

celebration occurring between January 21 and February 19. The dates change from year to year, like Easter.

The Lantern Festival is on the first day of the full moon following the Chinese New Year. During the Lantern Festival, children carry candlelit lanterns in the street.

If you or your child is fascinated with China, Chinese food, or dragon parades, then you just might enjoy this party theme. Celebrate with Chinese food, costumes, kite making and games. Read on to see how to bring a little of the excitement of the Chinese New Year into your home, and get ready to go gung-ho!

☙ CHINESE PAPER ❧ FAN INVITATION

Write your party message out on the piece of 8½ × 11-inch paper. Write the message along just the top half of the 11-inch side. The following is an example of what to write on the paper: "It's a Chinese New Year Party! Please come help us celebrate. We will make some great Chinese crafts, play Chinese games, eat Chinese food and have a great time! Hope you can make it!" Then write the date, time, place, and your phone number. Fold the paper accordion-style, lengthwise. Fold the end up and staple it at the fold. Fan out the folds, so that you can read the written message. You now have a fan! It is best to hand-deliver the invitation, but it may be mailed. You can also make an invitation on your computer and print a dragon on it. Write the message as with the paper fan. You might also check with party supply stores and Oriental stores to see if they carry Chinese New Year invitations.

☙ DECORATIONS ❧

The Chinese people believe that the color red scares away evil spirits. Red is a lucky color for the Chinese. It is also believed that red is the color of happiness.

- Hang red balloons and crepe paper streamers from the mailbox, front porch and in the party area.

- Hang a "Happy Chinese New Year" good luck sign on the front door. Purchase one or make it out of red construction paper with black lettering. Check your local Oriental market for an item called a door guard. It's a picture that guards your door from evil spirits and protects it from letting them enter.

- Make signs on red paper with black ink, that read "Long Life" and "Luck Has Arrived."

- Hang paper Chinese decorations, traditional Chinese lanterns and kites from the ceiling. You may be able to find these at Oriental stores and party supply stores.

- Hang a picture of the current animal of the new year's zodiac. If it is "The Year of the Dragon," hang a picture of an Oriental type of dragon. If it is "The Year of the Horse," hang a picture of a horse, etc.

- Hang pictures or maps of China. Check with a travel agent for brochures.

- Decorate your home with cherry blossom flowers and mums (you may need to use silk flower stems).

- Hang Chinese papier-mâché masks on the walls in the party area.

- Hang pictures of firecrackers made of construction paper or printed on a computer.

- For placemats, use paper Chinese placemats. Ask a restaurant if you may buy some. Use Chinese paper fans as placecards and paint each child's name on the wooden or plastic handle. Another placecard idea is to use Confucius sayings. Check out a book from your local library or check the Internet for information on Confucius sayings. Guests old enough to read should get a kick out of them. They will ask you what the sayings mean, so be prepared to explain. Some good Confucius quotes are: "Study the past, if you would divine the future"; "The superior man acts before he speaks, and afterward speaks"; "What you do not want done to yourself, do not do to others."

- For a table centerpiece, decorate the table with stacks of apples and oranges in the shape of a pyramid. Place a book on the Chinese New Year on the table for guests to look at, or read it to them.

- Burn Chinese incense. Just keep it out of curious hands' reach.

- Fireworks are thought to scare away evil spirits in the year to come. Have a few real firecrackers to light, but keep children at a safe distance. Check your local fire codes to see if fireworks are legal.

- If you have traditional Chinese clothing, wear it.

- Play Oriental music (check your local library, Oriental store, or music store). Play the song "Kung Fu Fighting" (Carl Douglas).

🎉 FOOD 🎉

If you do not have time to cook, have a good friend or relative pick up Chinese food from a local restaurant, or have it delivered. Call the restaurant before the day of the party to place the order, and call again the day of the party to confirm the order. Purchased wrapped chopsticks at an Oriental store or a restaurant supply store. You could even save the unopened ones that you may receive from an Oriental restaurant, or ask the manager if you may purchase some. See Easy Chopsticks to make a pair that are easy for children to use. Below are some ideas of what you could serve. There are many more ideas than you can possibly use, so you will have to pick which you like best.

- Dumplings: The Chinese hide a candy prize in one dumpling. The one who gets the candy is said to have good luck in the coming year.

- Stir-fry: Duck, chicken and goose are the favorite holiday meats.

- Won ton soup

- Egg rolls

- Chinese noodles: Asians associate noodles with long life and prosperity. The longer the noodle, the longer your life.

- Rice: Mounds of rice are a symbol of hope for a good harvest in the coming year.

- Eggs — dyed red: The egg is the symbol of life and red is the color of celebration.

- Oranges and apples stacked in pyramids: Mandarin oranges are a favorite snack.

- Walnuts and hazelnuts

- Chinese fortune cookies or almond cookies

- Ice cream or sherbet: The Chinese invented ice cream.

• Chinese green tea: The Chinese invented tea.

Easy Chopsticks

When my children go to our favorite Chinese restaurant, the waitress always hands them the following version of chopsticks. For a small child who cannot eat easily with chopsticks, these work great. But remind the children that in China it is considered bad manners to point or wave your chopsticks.

You will need:

A set of chopsticks with a paper wrapper, 1 per guest
A rubber band, 1 per guest

What to do:

1. Place the two chopsticks together and wrap them tightly on the end that you hold with the rubber band.

2. Fold up the paper wrapper that comes with the chopsticks, making it about ½-inch wide.

3. Slide it in between the chopsticks down to the end with the rubber band. This will form a tweezers-like eating utensil that is fun to use.

Chinese Dragon Cake

You will need:

Two 8- or 9- inch round baked cakes
6 cups white frosting
Green food coloring

One regular marshmallow, for the eye
1 chocolate chip, red hot or piece of chocolate, for the pupil
Dark chocolate candy bars or candy corn, for the scales
Red string licorice, for the tongue

What to do:

1. Bake and cool the cakes as directed. Cut the cakes as shown in illustration (fig. 2a & b). If desired, freeze the cake pieces uncovered for about 1 hour to make frosting spread easier.

2. Remove the cakes from the freezer and position as illustration shows (fig. 2c) on a foil-covered 20 × 36-inch board.

3. Frost the entire cake with light green tinted frosting, reserving about ¾ cup for decorating.

4. Slice the marshmallow in half and position for the eye. Put a little bit of light green frosting over the top half of the eye as an eyelid. Use the chosen piece of candy for the pupil.

5. Tint the remaining frosting a darker green. Fill a frosting bag with the dark green frosting and fit with a round tip. Pipe scales on the dragon's body as shown in the illustration (fig. 2c).

6. Cut triangle scales out of the chocolate bars or use candy corn to insert down the back and tail.

7. Place red licorice as if it were fire coming out of the dragon's mouth.

8. Put a chocolate chip or a piece of chocolate on the end of the nose for a nostril.

Umbrella Cupcakes

If time is short, bake a batch of cupcakes and simply stick a paper umbrella into each one. Paper umbrellas can be found in the mixed drink aisle of a grocery store, or at an Oriental restaurant.

🎉 ARRIVAL 🎉 OF GUESTS

Teach your guests how to say Happy New Year in Chinese, by greeting them at the door and saying, "Gung Bay Fat Chow." They may look at you quite strangely at first — that is, until

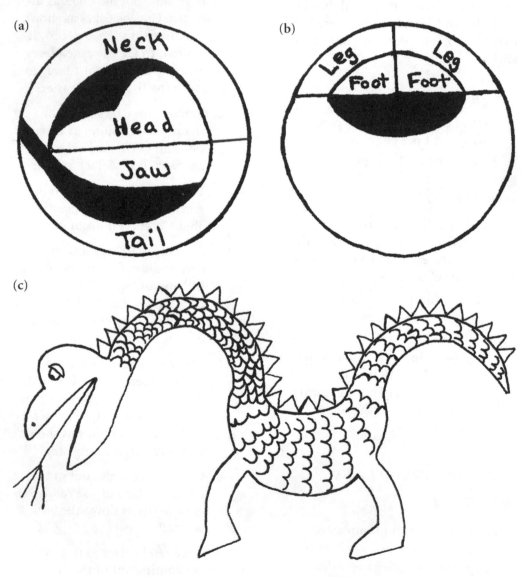

Fig. 2. Chinese Dragon Cake

you explain the meaning of what you have just said.

⚑ CRAFTS ⚑

Shadow Puppets

These puppets first became a form of entertainment in China, India and other Far Eastern countries. No one is quite sure when they came to be. The first written record comes from the tenth century, about a thousand years ago. It is believed that they date back much longer than that. Shadow puppets probably evolved around the time the Chinese invented paper during the Han Dynasty (2006 B.C.–A.D. 220). Early shadow puppets were made of paper. Later, puppets were made of leather. It is very likely that shadowgraphs (hand shadows reflected on a wall or cave) may go back to prehistoric times.

You will need:

Cardboard

Scissors

A hole puncher

Glue, tape or stapler

Sticks: paint stirrers, craft sticks, wooden dowels, straws, bamboo sticks, or even whittled tree sticks

A bright flashlight

A bare wall

What to do:

1. Lay all of the supplies out on a table and let the children cut out any shape or figure that they choose from a piece of cardboard (e.g., dragons, humans, dogs, cats, ghosts, etc.). Use the hole puncher for the eyes and mouths. Glue, tape or staple the figures to the stick.

2. Turn out the lights and draw the curtains, if necessary. Let two children at a time take turns standing near a wall, as you shine the flashlight at their puppets. Adjust the distance from the wall, if necessary. The puppets should cast a much larger shadow of the actual cardboard figure. If the children like, let them tell a story or put on a quick play, or they can just admire the figures on the wall by moving them.

Variation: If time is limited, just do hand shadows on the wall. One good book to get on the subject is *Shadowgraphs Anyone Can Make* by Phila H. Webb and Jane Corby.

Chinese Paper Fans

See Chinese Paper Fan Invitation.

Origami

Origami is the Oriental art of paper folding, which developed into a traditional Japanese craft. The Chinese were the first to discover paper. They too are very skilled at making things out of paper. Take out a book from the library or buy a book on the art of origami paper folding, and show the children some interesting things that you can make out of paper. Some things that can be made are boats that actually sail, birds that flap their wings, planes that fly, or even frogs that jump as shown below.

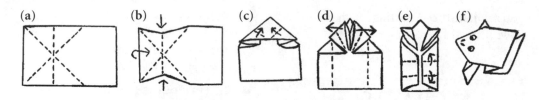

Fig. 3. Origami Jumping Frog

Origami Jumping Frog

You will need:

3- × 5-inch index cards (if you can find green ones, that would be great), 1 per guest

What to do:

1. Fold the top 3 inches over crossways. First to the left, then unfold. Next to the right, then unfold. This will create an "X"-shaped crease. See illustration (fig. 3a).

2. Fold the paper over at the center of the "X," or about 1½ inches from the edge of the paper.

3. Push in sides of the card at the crease and smooth down the resulting triangular form. (See fig. 3b.)

4. Make all folds shown in illustration (fig. 3c, d & e), turn figure over, and draw on a face.

5. To make the frog jump, push down gently on its back with your finger, then slide your finger off and watch the frog jump!

Chinese Mask

Make these easy masks out of paper plates by cutting out two oval shapes for the eyes before the day of the party. During the party, allow the children to draw on faces with felt-tipped markers as the illustration shows (fig. 4).

Fig. 4. Chinese Mask

Fish Kites

Kite flying is quite popular throughout Asia and is linked to many ancient traditions. The Chinese also used kites to send messages along the Great Wall of China. Paper kites in the shape of carps like the one illustrated (fig. 5) are hung outside of homes by Japanese children during the Children's Day celebration (May 5) in Japan. When the wind blows through the kites, they appear as if they are fish swimming. The carp stands for energy, strength, and a long life.

You will need:

Scissors

Paper or fabric

Felt-tip markers

A hole puncher

Strips of cardboard and a cardboard fish shaped template

Glue

String

Bamboo sticks, wooden dowels, or even straight sticks from your yard

What to do:

1. Fold a square of paper or fabric over to form a rectangle. Let the children trace the fish-shaped template on the paper or fabric with a felt-tip marker. The outline of the fish template shape should look like the shape of the illustration shown (fig. 5).

2. Show the children how to draw scales and fins on the fish shapes with the felt-tip markers.

3. Glue the sides of the fish together. Be sure to leave the mouth and tail ends open so the wind can blow through the kite.

4. Use thin precut strips of cardboard to fit around the inside of the mouth, creating a ring shape. Using the hole puncher, cut two holes, one on each side of the mouth. Glue in place and allow to dry.

5. Thread string through the holes in the mouth, and attach the other end to a stick or a dowel. You now have a windsock ready to swim in the breeze!

Caution: Keep away from power lines.

Fig. 5. Fish Kite

🎉 GAMES AND 🎉 ACTIVITIES

Games That Children Like to Play in China

Children in China like to play hopscotch, marbles, ping-pong, cat's cradle, skip rope, and five stones (like jacks). Consider playing one of these games, or if you have a small group play a game of Chinese checkers.

Yo-Yo Tricks

The first yo-yos appeared in China around 1000 B.C. They were made from ivory discs and silk cords. The word yo-yo means "come back." When you stop and think that this toy has been around for about 3000 years, I suppose that says something for its popularity. Your guests should enjoy playing with this toy. Pass out yo-yos and let the children show one another fun tricks. If you, a relative, or a friend know any good tricks, show them to the children. If you like, hold a contest to see who can hold the longest spin. Time the children with a stopwatch or a watch secondhand. A contest such as this will have to be limited to children about 10 and over, since younger children can have a difficult time using a yo-yo.

Teach Some Chinese Language

Before the party, teach your child how to say a few of the following examples and you will have your guests speaking in Chinese too! It's fun!

English	Chinese
Hello	Nee how ("ow" as in "cow")
Please	Ching
Thank you	Shie shie ("I" as in "machine")
Good-bye	Dzi jen ("I" as in "bite")
Dragon	Loong

Take a Trip

Many karate and martial arts schools have party packages, and will be happy to hold a party for you. For many schools, it is a way to introduce new students to their school, and to show off their stuff, so to speak. If you like, take the guests back to your home afterwards for a party. Play the song "Kung Fu Fighting" and let the children show you some moves!

Chinese Dragon Parade

During the Chinese New Year Festival rockets, sizzlers, and other fireworks are set off to drive away the evil spirits of the old year. People perform what is known as the dragon dance in the streets while under a costume of a long dragon. In China, the dragon is a sign of good fortune. The dragon is said to have many feet so that it may carry lots of good luck to the Chinese in the New Year. A lion is also present. The lion's purpose is to scare away the old year. Have a dragon parade of your own. See below for details.

You will need:

An old sheet or a large amount of yellow material (with yellow fringes added, if desired)

Dragon mask: made of a piece of cardboard and painted

Chinese masks (see Crafts)

Spirited Oriental music

Chinese paper fans made (see Invitation) or purchased

Instruments for children to play: symbols, flutes, drums, pots and pans, etc.

What to do:

1. Choose about 3 children to play the "Dragon." The 3 children all get under the sheet or material, which resembles the dragon's long body. One child (the leader) holds the dragon mask. All three kneel down on the floor or ground and pretend that the dragon is sleeping.

2. Choose a few other children to wake the dragon. They do this by gently tapping the "Dragon" on his back with their paper fans.

3. Give the remaining children their instruments. As the "Dragon" wakes up they begin playing their instruments and parading around the room. Play the Oriental music at this point.

4. Any other remaining children hold their masks to their faces. All of the children parade around the room like a dragon would to the music.

Chinese Relay

You will need:

Several newspapers or sticks
Masking tape or rubber bands

What to do:

1. If using newspaper, assemble them into sticks before the party. Roll newspapers lengthwise, tightly. Fasten with masking tape or rubber bands. Make 16 rolls.

2. During the party, lay down two rows of newspaper or sticks, 8 rolls in each row and about 2 feet apart.

3. Divide the children into two equal teams and have them stand in rows behind their newspaper or sticks.

4. At the signal to go, the first child in each line must hop over each newspaper or stick without touching it, turn around, and hop back over them.

5. He then touches off the next child in line and that player does the same. This continues until one of the teams finishes. The first team to finish wins.

Chinese Chicken

This game is played the same as Chinese Relay. The only difference is,

once all of each team finish, then the "first" player must again hop forward over all of the rolls or sticks. When he reaches the last roll or stick he must kick it away and hop back. When he gets to the other end, he again kicks away the last roll or stick. He continues on back and forth until all of his team's rolls or sticks have been kicked. The first child to finish wins for his whole team. You will need to choose someone very energetic to be first in line for this game. It just may be the right game to burn off his enormous amount of energy!

Chinese Get-Up

Have everyone choose a partner and sit on the ground or floor, back to back, and lock their arms together. At the signal to go, the partners must try to stand on their feet without unlocking their arms. The two partners to be the first to their feet win.

Crab Walk Race

You will need:

2 garden hoses, string or masking tape

What to do:

1. Set the hose, string or masking tape on the ground or floor in two equal zigzag lines.

2. Divide the children into two equal teams and have them stand single file at the end of the zigzag line. Have the first two children in line get down on the ground. Have them put their hands behind their backs and have their feet pointed toward the other children.

3. At the signal to go, they must race backwards like a crab on all fours toward the goal.

4. As soon as the first team member gets to the "end of the line," the next child in line must begin to do the same as the first child. The next child in line may not go before the first child reaches the end. As soon as the second child reaches the end, the next child goes and so on. The first team to have all of its team members complete the task wins.

Catch the Dragon's Tail

Line the children up single file. Each child must place their hands on the shoulders of the child in front of them. The child at the front of the line must try to tag the child at the end of the line. The children in the middle sway the line and curve it so that the child at the front of the line cannot tag the child at the back of the line. When the child at the front of the line succeeds, he then gets to go to the end of the line as the tail. The next child in line then becomes the child at the front to catch the dragon's tail. Continue playing in this manner until every child has had a turn to be at the front of the line, or as long as time allows.

Chinese Chopsticks Relay

You will need:

2 sets of chopsticks

2 balls, such as lightweight plastic balls or tennis balls

What to do:

1. Mark a start line, and mark a goal line 20–30 feet away. Divide the children into two teams and have them stand behind the start line. Hand the first child in each line two chopsticks. They place the ball between their chopsticks and hold it tightly.

2. At the signal to go, they run to the goal and back. If they drop the ball, they must pick it back up, place it between the chopsticks and continue.

3. When they return to their team they pass the ball and chopsticks to the next child in line. He does the same. This continues until the first team has all of their players finish first. That team wins.

Variation: If you have one set of chopsticks for each child, have the children stand in a line and pass the ball to one another, using the chopsticks. The first team to get the ball all the way down the line and then back again wins.

The Great Wall of China

The Great Wall of China is the longest wall in the world. It is 2,150 miles long. It was built to keep out the Mongolian invaders from the north, but didn't always do so. The real Great Wall of course is very long, but this wall will be very tall. To play this game, see Cinco de Mayo Festival/Mexican Fiesta game Aztec and Mayan Ruins.

Ping-Pong Blowing Contest

You will need:

Ping-pong balls, 1 per guest
Masking tape or string

What to do:

1. Make two lines with the tape or string and place them three feet apart. Have all of the children kneel along one line and set their balls on the line.

2. At the signal to go, each player tries to blow his ping-pong ball across the other line of tape or string. The first child to cross the line wins.

Chinese Zodiac

The Chinese New Year marks the beginning of a 12-year cycle. Each year has its symbolic creature. Many Chinese believe that the year of a person's birth is the primary factor in determining that person's personality traits, physical and mental characteristics, and degree of success and happiness throughout his lifetime. There are many legends surrounding the origination of the Chinese New Year, but one popular story that is passed on tells of Buddha asking all of the animals on Earth to join him for dinner before he leaves the planet. Only 12 animals show up, those being the animals of the Chinese zodiac. In appreciation, Buddha gives each of these animals their own year in the Chinese calendar.

To obtain a current Chinese zodiac, visit a local Chinese restaurant; many use paper placemats that have the zodiac printed on it. Take one home after your meal. You may also get a book on the subject at a bookstore, Oriental store or library. The following is an example of the Chinese zodiac. To learn which animal sign is your child's or guest's, find the year of birth among the 12 signs, or add or subtract 12 from the year of birth to find the animal sign. For some of us older folks, we may need to add 12 more than once or twice!

Year	
1988, 2000, 2012	The Year of the Dragon: You are eccentric and your life is complex. You have a very passionate nature and good health.
1989, 2001, 2013	The Year of the Snake: Wise and intense with a tendency towards physical beauty, but vain.
1990, 2002, 2014	The Year of the Horse: Popular and attractive. Often pretentious and impatient.
1991, 2003, 2015	The Year of the Sheep or Goat: Elegant and creative. You are timid and prefer anonymity.
1992, 2004, 2016	The Year of the Monkey: Very intelligent and able to influence others. An enthusiastic achiever, but easily discouraged.
1993, 2005, 2017	The Year of the Cock or Rooster: Devoted to work

and seeks knowledge. Selfish and eccentric.

1994, 2006, 2018   The Year of the Dog: Loyal, honest and works well with others. Generous, yet stubborn.

1995, 2007, 2019   The Year of the Pig or Boar: Noble and chivalrous. Your friends will be lifelong, yet you are prone to marital conflict.

1996, 2008, 2020   The Year of the Rat: Ambitious and honest, but prone to spend freely.

1997, 2009, 2021   The Year of the Ox: Bright, patient and inspiring to others. Would be an outstanding parent, yet you could be happy by yourself.

1998, 2010, 2022   The Year of the Tiger: Tiger people are aggressive, courageous, candid, and sensitive.

1999, 2011, 2023   The Year of the Rabbit or Hare: Luckiest of all signs. Talented, articulate, and affectionate. Tend to be shy and seek peace.

Shoe Scramble

This may be a good game to play near the end of the party, to get everyone to put on their shoes, if they have taken them off. Seat all of the children in a circle and have them place their shoes in a pile in the center of the circle. At a signal to go, they all rush to find their own pair of shoes. The first one to find their shoes and put them on wins.

Note: Don't play this game if two guests have the same exact type of shoes, unless the shoes are labeled with masking tape. It may cause confusion.

♟ FAVOR AND ♟ PRIZE IDEAS

For a favor holder, use Chinese paperboard carryout food cartons. Try to get the type that fold up into a box with the little carry handle. Check with a restaurant or a restaurant supply store to see if they have some that you may buy. The following are some filler suggestions: fortune cookies, plastic ninja warrior figures, small stuffed panda bears, costume jewelry pearl necklaces (real pearl necklaces are worn during the festival), toy dragons, Buddha necklaces, red Chinese New Year money envelopes called leisee (lay-*see*), found in Oriental stores, stuffed with candy or a "lucky" coin (half dollars, Chinese coins or gold foil-covered chocolate coins), Chinese paper fans (see Crafts or purchase inexpensive ones), Chinese zodiacs, Oriental straw hats, papier mâché masks, Chinese Masks (see Crafts), Origami animals (see Crafts), kites, yo-yos, or shadow puppets (see Crafts).

Valentine's Day Party

• *February 14* •

February 14 brings thoughts of love, friendship, cupid's arrow, Valentine cards and candy. This holiday is named after St. Valentine, the Roman priest and martyr, known as the patron of lovers. The customs that are traditionally practiced on his feast day have no connection with his life, but are thought to be related to the Ancient Roman festival Lupercalia. At that festival for sweethearts, Roman girls put their names in a love urn and the boys drew a girl's name from the urn. The name that was drawn was the name of the girl to be their partner at the festival. The early Christian church transferred this popular pagan custom to the St. Valentine's feast day, and I'm sure that there are many children and adults today who are glad for that. Just imagine if it hadn't been kept, as many pagan holidays weren't.

In honor of this holiday, let your family and friends know how much you love and care for them with a Valentine's Day celebration. Read this chapter for some "love"ly ideas to make your party special!

VALENTINE'S HEART INVITATION

There are many ways that you can make this invitation. The illustration (fig. 6a & b) shown is simple to make. You can use a stencil or a cookie cutter to trace a heart shape onto the paper, and then cut out the shape. Write words, such as the words illustrated. If desired, dress up the invitation by cutting the heart into a folded card and gluing the back of the invitation to a

31

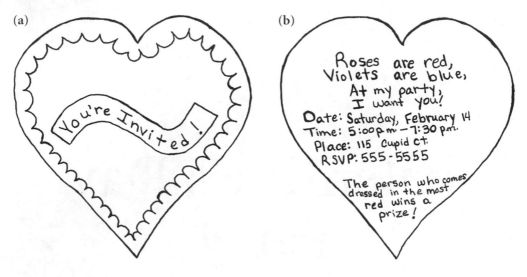

Fig. 6. Valentine's Heart Invitation

white paper doily. You could even add a bow made of ribbon to the top of the invitation. Another idea is to cut out one smaller shaped heart and one larger shaped heart. Glue the smaller heart to the center of the larger heart. Yet another idea is to use a computer to print several hearts onto the front of an invitation. Ask your guests to come dressed in red. Tell them that the child with the most red on wins a prize.

☃ DECORATIONS ☃

- Hang red, pink and white balloons and crepe paper streamers from the mailbox, front porch and in the party area.

- Put a large heart on the front door that reads "Happy Valentine's Day!" Make one out of red or pink construction paper, or purchase one. Decorations can be found at many stores near this holiday.

- Hang curled red, pink and white ribbon from doorways, ceilings and chairs.

- Hang pictures of Cupid, arrows and hearts around the house. Make heart shapes to resemble Valentine candy. If you have a heart shaped cake pan, use it to trace the heart shapes on construction paper. Write things like "Luv Ya," "Be Mine," "My Pal" or "You're Tops."

- Use a red tablecloth and pink tableware (or vice versa). You can also purchase Valentine tableware.

- Use white doilies for placemats and place a wrapped candy heart on each one.

- For placecards, have your child write what it is that they like about each guest on a paper heart that is folded like a card. Stand the card up at each child's place setting; they will enjoy reading these.

- Place a bowl of Valentine candy or a vase of red roses in the center of the table. Give each guest a flower to take home at the end of the party.

- If you can find heart-shaped balloons, tie one to each child's chair. Stick a surprise in each before inflating. When everyone is seated, and finished eating, pop the balloons to give everyone a surprise.

- Play songs that contain the word "love" in the lyrics. Some good songs are "Cupid" (Sam Cooke — found on the CD "The Best of Sam Cooke"), "Get Together" (The Youngbloods), "If I Had a Hammer (The Hammer Song)" (Peter, Paul & Mary), "Love Gets Me Every Time" (Shania Twain), "Love Me Do" (The Beatles), "She Loves You" (The Beatles), "Don't Go Breaking My Heart" (Elton John & Kiki Dee), "Love Rules" (The Kinleys), "Crazy Little Thing Called Love" (Queen) or "All Shook Up" (Elvis Presley).

🎉 FOOD 🎉

- Heart Sandwiches: Peanut butter (or cream cheese) and strawberry jelly sandwiches cut with a heart shaped cookie cutter. If possible, purchase pink colored bread, sometimes found during this time of year.

- Fresh strawberries or chocolate covered strawberries

- Carrot sticks or chips

- Valentine's Punch: One bottle of strawberry/cranberry juice mixed with one 2-liter bottle of ginger ale.

Heart Cake

Heart shaped cake pans can be found in many craft stores and kitchen supply stores, but if you prefer, make one as described below without a heart shaped pan.

You will need:

One box of cake mix for 2-layer cake, plus ingredients as box directs
3–4 cups white frosting
Red food coloring
1 cake doily (found at craft and kitchen supply stores), optional

What to do:

1. Mix the cake mix as directed. Pour half of the batter (about 2¼ cups) into an 8-inch round cake pan and pour the remaining batter into an 8-inch square pan. If you don't have an 8-inch round pan, a 9-inch round cake can be trimmed to fit. Bake and cool as directed.

2. When cool, cut the round cake in half and position it next to the square cake on top of a doily as shown in illustration on next page (fig. 7b).

3. Frost the cake with 3 cups of white frosting, or color 3 cups of the frosting pink. Color any remaining frosting with red food coloring, and pipe on a red or pink border at the top and the bottom of the cake, using a star frosting tip and a decorator's bag. If desired, frost roses on the top of the cake.

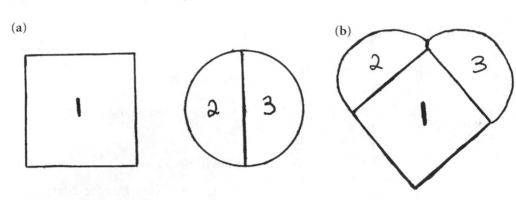

Fig. 7. Heart Cake

Heart Cupcakes

These cupcakes are very simple to make if time is short.

You will need:

1 box of cake mix, plus ingredients as box directs
24 paper or foil cupcake liners
Aluminum foil
One 16-oz. can or 2 cups white icing
Red food coloring
Heart shaped candy

What to do:

1. Line a muffin pan with the baking cups. Place a small rolled ball of foil between the liner and the pan, pressing in toward the center creating a heart shape of the liner.

2. Prepare the cake mix as directed, and pour into paper cups. Bake and cool as directed.

3. Frost the cupcakes white, or color the frosting pink with red food coloring. Color any remaining frosting pink or red to frost on a border of a different color than the cupcakes. Frost on a shell or star border along the top edge of each cupcake, using a small star frosting tip.

4. Place one heart shaped candy in the center of each cupcake.

🎉 CRAFTS 🎉

Chocolate Roses

These pretty little roses make great party favors or prizes. If you like, make them before the day of the party, place them in a flower vase as a decoration and give one to each guest to take home at the end of the party.

You will need:

A 5 × 5-inch square of red cellophane or clear red plastic wrapping
2 red foil wrapped Hershey Kisses
1 artificial silk leaf
1 9-inch long piece of floral wire
Green floral tape

What to do:

1. Place the two Hershey Kisses

together, with the round ends touching, in the center of the red square of cellophane or plastic wrapping as illustrated (fig. 8). Wrap the cellophane or plastic wrapping around the two Hershey Kisses tightly and gather it at the tip of one of the candies. Twist the cellophane or plastic wrapping tightly.

2. Place the wrapped candy on top of the artificial silk leaf, placing the gathered end of cellophane or plastic wrapping on top of the stem of the leaf.

3. Place the floral wire on top of the twisted cellophane or plastic wrapping.

4. Wrap the floral tape around the gathered plastic wrapping, artificial leaf stem and the floral wire, securing all together to prevent it from un-raveling. Continue wrapping the floral tape all down the length of the floral wire to appear as a rose stem. You now have a chocolate rose!

Fig. 8.
Chocolate Rose

Heart Shaped Picture Frame

For parties with younger children, you may want to make the frames before the party and let the children decorate them with decorations.

You will need:

Thin cardboard

A heart shaped stencil or a large heart shaped cookie cutter to trace

Scissors

Fabric remnants (check bargain tables at fabric stores)

Fleece (found at fabric stores)

Fabric glue (found at craft and fabric stores)

Pens, 1 per guest (if the children will be making the frames themselves)

Optional items for decorating: lace, ribbon, ribbon roses, silk flowers, bead strands, etc.

A Polaroid camera and film, or a digital camera, optional

What to do:

1. Before the party, trace 2 heart shapes for each guest onto the cardboard. If your stencil is not large enough, you may trace it onto paper and enlarge the picture with a copy machine or a fax machine.

2. Cut out the heart shapes from the cardboard. Cut out a round hole from the center of "half" of the heart shapes in the size that you would like your pictures to be. See illustration on next page (fig. 9a). This will be the front of frame.

3. Cut out one picture frame stand from the cardboard for each picture frame.

4. During the party, lightly apply glue to one side of the front

piece (or the piece with the hole). Place the glue side down on a square of fleece that is slightly larger than the heart shape. Trim fleece around all edges, including the center cutout.

5. Lightly apply a few drops of glue along the fleece edges. Place the fleece side down on a square of fabric that is slightly larger than the heart frame (at least ½–1 inch larger). Using a pen, trace about ½-inch from the edge of the front of the frame including the center cutout. Cut along the trace lines. Clip the ½-inch edge about every ⅓-inch, and about ¹⁄₁₆-inch away from the edge of the front. This is done to prevent the fabric from bunching when it is pulled around the frame to the back-side.

6. Apply a line of glue along the back edges of the cardboard. Wrap the fabric around to the backside.

7. Follow steps 5 and 6 to make a back piece for the frame with a solid heart shape, excluding the center cutout.

8. Apply fabric to the stand by gluing it on and trimming away any excess material. Fold the stand as illustration shows (fig. 9b) and apply glue to the upper edge. Attach the stand to the back of the frame, position-ing it so that the point of the heart is even with the stand.

9. At this point, younger children

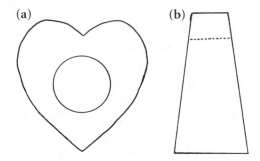

Fig. 9. Heart Picture Frame

may finish the frame by deco-rating the front of it.

10. Take a picture of the children and trim it to fit inside of the frame, if necessary. Apply glue to the inside edges of the frame and place the picture in the window or hole part of the frame. Press the front and the back piece together and your frame is done!

🎉 GAMES AND 🎉 ACTIVITIES

Love Stories

Hand each child a piece of paper and a pencil, and ask them to write the funniest love story that they can think of. It can be about anyone: Cupid, themselves, their best friends, their pet, their teacher or even an alien. Give them some goofy ideas to work with. Tell them the funnier the better. After everyone has had a chance to finish their story, let them take turns reading the stories aloud. Encourage everyone to applaud each story after it is finished being read. Award a prize for the story that receives the most applause. Be sure to video this. You will want to listen to it for years to come.

Variation: Sit the guests in a circle. Hand the first child a piece of paper and a pencil. The child writes the first line of a love story, and then he passes the paper to a child to the right of him. The next child looks at what has been written, then he adds the next line. Remind them the crazier the better. Fold the paper after each new line is added so that only the last line can be read. Continue passing the paper around the circle as long as you like. Have someone write a good ending, possibly the last child. The resulting story should be hilarious.

Who Stole My Heart?

This game is played much like Doggy Doggy Where's Your Bone. The words have just been changed.

You will need:

One heart shape cut out of red posterboard

What to do:

1. Choose one child to sit in a chair with his back to the rest of the children. Put the heart under his chair. Have all of the other children sit on the floor behind the chair.

2. Ask the child in the chair to cover his eyes with his hands. While his eyes are covered, choose one of the other children to sneak up and very quietly "steal" his heart. No one must talk or make sounds.

3. The child who has stolen the heart returns to his original

spot and hides the heart behind his back. The other players pretend to be hiding the heart also. At this point all join in saying, "Cupid, Cupid where's my heart? Did you shoot it with your dart?"

4. This is the sitting child's cue to turn around. He gets three guesses as to which child he thinks stole his heart. If all three guesses are incorrect, the child with the heart gets a turn in the chair. But if he guesses correctly, then he gets another turn in the chair. Try to play until all of the children have had a turn in the chair, or as long as time allows.

Spin the Bottle

You will need:

An empty soda bottle
Chocolate candy kisses
A bowl
Numbered cards, 1 per guest

What to do:

1. Seat all of the players in a circle and give them each a number and a candy kiss. Ask them to remember their number and not to eat the candy kiss.

2. An adult then calls out a number and then spins the bottle on its side.

3. When the mouth of the bottle spins in front of the child whose number is called, he must catch it before it stops spinning. If he doesn't catch it, he must then forfeit his candy

kiss and toss it in the bowl. He is then out of the game. The game continues in this manner until only one child is left with a candy kiss. He is the winner and gets to keep all of the candy kisses.

Heart Hunt

You will need several hearts made out of red and pink construction paper and one gold heart. The gold heart may be a piece of cardboard spray painted gold. Hide all of the hearts around the inside or outside of the house. At the signal to go, all search for the hearts. Award a prize to the child who finds the most hearts and one to the child who finds the gold heart. Valentine candy would be an appropriate prize.

Cupid's Arrow Archery

You will need:

A large piece of cardboard approximately 30 inches square

Paint or felt tip markers

A bow and arrow with a rubber tip or a sponge tip

An ink pad

What to do:

1. Before the party, draw or paint a large heart on the cardboard. Within the heart draw a target, with circles one within the other. On the inner circle write "Gotcha." On the next circle write "Close, but no cigar"; the next circle "Ahh rats"; the next

"Better luck next time" and the outside circle "Afraid of cooties."

2. During the party, prop the target up in a place where you will not be concerned about ink getting on the furniture or the floor. A garage, basement or outdoors may be best.

3. Line the children up, and allow them to take a shot at being Cupid by shooting the arrow at the target. As each child takes a turn shooting at the target, dip the rubber or foam tip in the ink pad, so that it will be easy to see what's been hit. Anyone hitting the center target wins a prize. An appropriate prize would be an inexpensive bow and arrow set or a package of Valentine candy with a picture of Cupid on it.

🎉 FAVOR AND 🎉 PRIZE IDEAS

Valentine heart-shaped candy, small box of chocolates, red candy licorice, Hershey Kisses, heart shaped items (e.g., stickers, erasers, balloons, pins, jewelry, note pads, stencils, etc.), red roses (see Decorations), Chocolate Roses (see Crafts), Valentine cards, or bottles of love pills (red hot candies placed in small spice jars or baby food jars and labeled "love pills").

Mardi Gras Party

• *Falls sometime between* • *February 3 and March 9*

Mardi Gras is carnival time in many places and it is New Orleans' legendary holiday. It is a time for parties, feasts, street parades and formal masquerade balls. The celebration marks the beginning of Lent (a Catholic time of prayer and sacrifice) and is an ancient custom that originated in southern Europe. The French brought Mardi Gras to Louisiana. It serves as a reminder of the story of Jesus' fast in the wilderness. Mardi Gras day is scheduled on a different date each year and is set to occur 46 days before Easter (the 40 days of Lent plus six Sundays). It can fall as early as February 3 or as late as March 9. Mardi Gras can occur on any Tuesday between these dates. The fluctuating date was established by the Catholic Church.

Mardi Gras is French for "Fat Tuesday"—fat because people used to eat up any eggs, fat, and butter in the house before giving them up for Lent,

and Tuesday because it always falls on the Tuesday before Ash Wednesday.

During Mardi Gras in New Orleans and Rio de Janeiro, Brazil, there are very colorful processions with people having as much fun as possible before Lent. There is spirited music, singing, and dancing. Many of the processionists wear elaborate costumes and masks. There is no general theme for Mardi Gras, but each individual parade follows a certain theme. Some of the popular parade themes are history, geography, entertainment, famous people, children's stories, mythology, legends and literature. Collectible trinkets (bead necklaces, cups and doubloons) and candy are thrown to the crowds from the elaborate parade floats.

The appeal of Mardi Gras extends far beyond New Orleans and Brazil, and is now celebrated by people all over. Invite some revelers over to your place this Mardi Gras and bring some of the thrill and excitement of the Mardi Gras celebration into your home — Louisiana style!

🎉 MARDI GRAS 🎉 MASK INVITATION

Make your invitations in mask shapes as illustrated (fig. 10a & b) on colorful construction paper. Cut two oval shapes out of contrasting colors of construction paper for the eyeholes and glue them in place on the front of the invitation. Spread a little glue on the front of the invitation and sprinkle it with glitter. If desired, glue colorful

metallic sequins onto the front of the invitation. If you will be hand delivering your invitations, you may want to glue some colorful feathers onto the front of the mask shape. On the back of the invitation your message could read, "In observance of the coming of Lent, we are having a Mardi Gras Party!" Write the date, time and place of the party. If you like, ask your guests to come dressed in a costume to disguise their identity. Tell your guests that they may come dressed as anything they like. They may wear an old Halloween costume, dance costume, or dress as a storybook character from a children's story. If you won't be making the craft Mardi Gras Masks, ask guests to come wearing one. At the end of the invitation write, "Ya'll come now!"

(a)

(b)

Fig. 10. Mardi Gras Mask Invitation

🎉 DECORATIONS 🎉

The official colors of Mardi Gras are purple, green and gold. Purple represents justice, green stands for faith and gold signifies power.

- Put very colorful crepe paper and balloons on your mailbox, front porch and in the party area.

- Place an opened, decorated umbrella, like the ones used in jazz parades, on your front porch or in the party area.

- Make or purchase pictures of King Neptune, King Crowns, Comedy/Tragedy (the happy and sad masks associated with drama), Mardi Gras jesters, paddlewheel steamboats, riverboats, street cars, alligators or swamps and hang them on the walls in the party area. These can be made on a computer printer.

- Make a sign that reads "French Quarter." You could use this sign to distinguish the area for the game Scavenger Hunt in the French Quarter.

- Hang up a map of the state of Louisiana or of the city New Orleans in the party area.

- Hang feathered masks on the walls in the party area.

- Hang a metallic shred curtain, usually found at party supply stores.

- Hang a banner that reads, "Happy Mardi Gras."

- If you have any instruments around your home such as a saxophone, a trumpet, an accordion, a fiddle, or a banjo, use it as a decoration in the party area.

- Use Mardi Gras themed tableware or bright green, yellow and purple colored tableware.

- For a centerpiece, place crumpled foil in the center of the table and throw brightly colored Metallic Mardi Gras necklaces over it. Throw confetti on the table, on and around the centerpiece.

- Hang a bull or ox shaped piñata from the ceiling in the party area.

- Play lively songs of Brazilian carnival music, Dixieland jazz, Swamp Pop, and French inspired Cajun and Creole/Zydeco music. One of my favorite Cajun CDs is "Cajun Party: Spicy Hot Music from Bayou Country" (sung by various artists). "Choo Choo Boogaloo" (Buckwheat Zy-

deco) is a good song to play. Children can't help but like this music!

♙ FOOD ♙

During Mardi Gras Creole and Cajun food is served. "Creole" is a term used to identify a blending of French, Spanish, African and Caribbean culture. "Cajun" is a term used to identify the French Acadians who settled in South Louisiana after their expulsion from Acadia (now Nova Scotia, Canada) in the 1700s. The Acadians mixed with mainland French immigrants, Spanish, English, German, Haitian, and Native Americans creating the distinctive and unique Cajun culture. The following menu ideas are some foods that come from these two cultures:

- Gumbo
- Jambalaya
- New Orleans Stew
- Red Beans and Rice
- Dirty Rice
- French Bread
- Bread Pudding
- Beignets ("Ben-yayz") — French-style doughnuts

King Cupcakes

Traditional Mardi Gras King Cakes are oval, sugared pastries that contain a doll hidden inside called a King Cake Baby. The person who finds the hidden doll is crowned "King" and must buy the next cake or throw the next Mardi Gras party. At some parties or restaurants a prize is awarded to the person finding the doll.

Bake a batch of cupcakes and then hide a King Cake Baby inside one of the cupcakes. To hide the King Cake Baby, cut a slit in the top of the cupcake and place it inside before frosting the cupcake. King Cake Babies can be found at many party supply stores during the Mardi Gras season. Frost the cupcakes with brightly colored purple, green and gold (or yellow) frosting.

Caution: Forewarn guests of the hidden doll. Since young children might choke on the King Cake Baby, place a gummy bear candy on top of each cupcake.

🎉 CRAFTS 🎉

Pie Plate Tambourines

You will need:

Aluminum disposable pie pans
A thin screwdriver
Twist ties or pieces of wire
Small objects that will make sounds when they bang against the pan: jingle bells, metal bottle tops with holes drilled in them, etc.
Ribbon

What to do:

1. Punch holes on the side of the plate with the screwdriver. Make sure that there are no sharp points sticking out, and remove any that could be harmful.

2. Use the twist ties or pieces wire to attach the small objects to the pie pan.

3. Attach ribbons for decoration.

Fiddles or Banjos

You will need:

Rubber bands
Empty tissue boxes
Cardboard
Stapler

What to do:

1. String the rubber bands over the opening of the tissue box.

2. If desired, add a handle onto the end by stapling on a long strip of cardboard. Let the children pluck away at their new stringed instruments for a Cajun music jam session!

Magazine Bead Necklaces

You will need:

Old magazines or glossy newspaper inserts
Scissors
A glue stick
Clean, new fishing line or thread
Plastic needles, if using thread

What to do:

1. Tear out bright, colorful pages from the magazines, and cut the pages into about 10½-inch long tapered strips that are about 1½ inches wide on one end and ½-inch wide on the other (almost like a stretched out triangle).

2. Starting at the wide end, tightly roll each strip to form a bead. Add a dab of glue to the end to hold the roll or "bead" in place. Allow the glue to dry at least five minutes. You can make these during the party or before the party, depending on the age of your guests.

3. Cut a piece of fishing line or thread to the length needed to make a necklace. Use the needles to string the beads onto the thread, or if using the fishing line, just push it through the holes. Tie the ends of the necklace together and clip off the excess thread or fishing line.

Mardi Gras Masks

You will need:

Plastic masquerade masks, 1 per guests (found at party supply stores)

Tubes of glitter glue

Metallic sequins or plastic gems

Craft feathers

Glue

Newspaper or a paper tablecloth

What to do:

1. Cover the work area with the newspaper or paper tablecloth to protect it.

2. Set out all of the materials on top of the newspaper or paper tablecloth. Pass out one mask to each guest and allow them to decorate their mask any way that they like.

Rattles or Maracas

See Cinco de Mayo/Mexican Fiesta Party Crafts, Maracas.

Face Painting

See St. Patrick's Day Party for Face Paint recipe. If you like, paint the children's faces to look like clown faces.

🎉 GAMES AND 🎉 ACTIVITIES

Hire Entertainment

Find a mummer who is really good with children. Ask him if you can go and see him perform elsewhere before hiring him for the party. If you are impressed, hire him to come and teach your guests some pantomime.

Hire a French storyteller to come and tell the children some fascinating stories. Some storytellers play musical instruments to help tell their stories. To find a French storyteller, check with your local cultural council.

Dance the Cajun Two-Step

Are you ready for a fais-do-do (street dance)? Now that your guests are all decked out for Mardi Gras and they have an instrument to play, show them how they dance in the Louisiana bayou! Get a video on Cajun culture from the library, and learn the Cajun two-step so that you can teach it to your guests. Bring out any musical instruments that you may have around your home along with the ones made during the party to spice things up a bit! Put on some exciting Cajun or Zydeco toe-tapping music and get your dancing feet ready to have some fun!

Torchlight Grand March

Flambeaux (or fueled torches) were at one time the only source of illumination at nighttime Mardi Gras parades. If your guests have come to the party all decked in costume, have a Torchlight Grand March, using flashlights as torches. If you like, tape red and yellow tissue paper flames to the flashlights. Let the children parade around as you video them strutting their stuff.

Costume Contest

Hold a costume contest. Award a prize to each guest for one of the following types of costumes: craziest, funniest, prettiest, most colorful, most unique, hardest to figure out, best disguise, most designs, etc.

Crowning Ceremony

Purchase or make two gold colored cardboard crowns. Choose a king and queen, picked from a random drawing, and hold a crowning ceremony.

Bead Toss

During the Mardi Gras parades, bead necklaces are thrown at the parade audiences.

You will need:

   1 regular bead necklace or a Mardi Gras bead necklace
   1 medium sized bucket

What to do:

1. Set the bucket on the floor and mark a throwing line about 8–10 feet away.

2. Line the children up behind the throwing line and give each a turn at throwing the necklace at the bucket. Anyone getting the necklace into the bucket wins a prize. This should not be too difficult to achieve, so have plenty of prizes on hand. An appropriate prize might be an inexpensive plastic bead necklace, candy necklace, or a piece of candy.

Alligators in the Bayou

You will need:

A 2 × 4 × 8 wood board (or a 1 × 6 × 8 wood board for younger guests)
Plastic toy alligators or paper alligators printed on a computer printer and cut out
Blindfold: a bandanna or scarf with a clothespin for securing

What to do:

1. Place the wood board on a level floor or ground.

2. Line the children up on one end of the board and have them take turns walking across the wood board while being blindfold. An adult will need to

stay close to the child walking across, and be ready to catch them should they lose their balance. Any child who can make it all the way across the wood board without falling off wins a prize. Everyone will think that this looks real easy – until they have had their turn! An appropriate prize would be a toy alligator, or something with an alligator theme.

Note: It will not be necessary to blindfold small children. Getting across without being blindfolded will still be a challenge for them.

Scavenger Hunt in the French Quarter

Novelty items: toy alligators, bead necklaces, plastic jewels, gold coins, doubloons, etc.

A list of the items hidden, 1 per child

What to do:

1. Before the party, hide the novelty items in a certain area of your house or yard. Set some of the items aside and do not hide them. If you have a pocket on your clothing, keep them in it.

2. During the party, pass out the lists of items hidden and the items unhidden (or in your pocket). Send everyone to search for them in an area that you will call "The French Quarter." If you see that someone hasn't found an item, make sure that you "inconspicuously" remove the hidden items from your pocket and place them where children who haven't found any items can see them. The idea is to make sure that everyone finds something and feels good.

3. After you feel that all of the items have been found, gather everyone in a circle and check off the items that have been found. Some items may not have been found. If time allows, send the children out to search for the remaining hidden items.

Bull or Ox Piñata

Since the Middle Ages, the bouef gras (a fatted bull or ox) has been the symbol of the last meat eaten before Lent. Today, a papier-mâché version is one of the Carnival's most recognizable symbols. Purchase or make a bull or ox shaped piñata for the children to break open during the party. See Holiday Piñatas for directions on how to make a Bull or Ox Piñata.

Teach Some French Language

English	French
Good morning/ Hello	Bonjour (bon jur)
Please	S'il vous plait (siv vou play)
Thank you	Merci (mare si)
Good-bye	au revoir (oh rev wahr)

♦ FAVOR AND ♦ PRIZE IDEAS

Mardi Gras theme items (e.g., coins, doubloons, balloons, shirt buttons, derby hats, bubble gum coins, stickers, tattoos, etc.), Mardi Gras bead necklaces, candy necklaces, glittery top hats, jester hats, king/queen crowns, party horns, plastic gold coins, plastic jewels, toy alligators, Pie Plate Tambourines (see Crafts), Fiddles and Banjos (see Crafts), Magazine Bead Necklaces (see Crafts), Mardi Gras Masks (see Crafts), or Rattles or Maracas (see Crafts), flashlights (see Activity, Torchlight Grand March).

St. Patrick's Day Party

• *March 17* •

Leapin' Leprechauns, it's St. Patrick's Day! This party is great fun for little lads and lasses! St. Patrick's Day is on March 17. Some say that this date marks the death of Bishop Patrick, who is the patron saint of Ireland, while others believe it is the day of his birth. No one knows for sure.

At the age of 16, Patrick was captured as a slave and taken from his home in England to Ireland. After six years, he escaped. He later returned to Ireland in A.D. 432, being sent by the Pope to convert the Irish people from their Druid beliefs to Christianity.

The green shamrock is so important to this holiday, because St. Patrick used it to explain the concept of the Trinity. Each leaf representing one of the following: The Father, the Son and the Holy Spirit. The shamrock grows all over Ireland, and is worn by Irish people as a symbol of their heritage.

The color green is also worn by people of all heritages on this holiday in the United States and Ireland. Anyone not wearing green may risk getting pinched by those who remembered to wear green.

The snakes are a part of the traditional holiday decorations, because it is believed that St. Patrick chased the snakes out of Ireland. It is said that he drove them into the sea and any serpent that touches Irish soil today will instantly die. This is only a legend, but the Irish will tell you that you can't find a snake in the whole island of Ireland. As far back as anyone can trace, snakes have never been found on the island. Lizards are the only reptiles found in Ireland.

Leprechauns are important to this holiday because Ireland is known as the home of fairies and leprechauns. Leprechauns are elves who mend the shoes of other fairies. They are usually rich and ill tempered. They keep their pots of gold hidden and disappear quickly. Finding a leprechaun wearing green is considered good luck. Wearing green on St. Patrick's Day is also considered good luck and is considered tradition. Since the color green is so important to this holiday, ask your guests to come to this party dressed in green, and award a prize to the person wearing the most green. A gold treasure hunt or a shamrock hunt is a must for this party.

With a wee bit of imagination and the ideas in this chapter, you are sure to have a great party. All little lads and lasses will go home from this party with their Irish eyes a smilin' (whether they have Irish ancestors to claim or not)!

♟ SHAMROCK ♟ INVITATION

Use a shamrock shaped cookie cutter or stencil to trace a shamrock shape onto a green piece of paper, and then cut out the shape. If the shape is not large enough, use a copy machine or a fax machine to enlarge the size. Write your message out as illustrated (fig. 11a & b). If you like, write your message as an Irish limerick. A limerick consists of five lines. The first two lines rhyme with the fifth and the third line rhymes with the fourth. If desired, add a line of glue around the border's edge and sprinkle some green glitter on it. You can also print the invitations on a computer printer using the words illustrated. Ask guests to come wearing

green. If you like, warn your guests that anyone not wearing green, especially on the actual St. Patrick's Day, may risk getting pinched. After all this is customary, but no one will really get pinched.

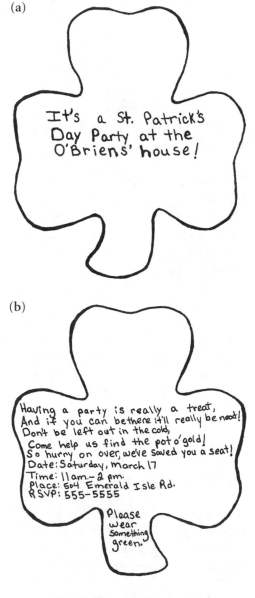

Fig. 11. Shamrock Invitation

🎉 DECORATIONS 🎉

- Decorate the mailbox, front porch and party area with green, yellow and white balloons and crepe paper streamers.

- Make a sign for your front yard that reads "Caution: Leprechaun Crossing."

- Put toy snakes near the front door, if you know your friends well enough that this won't send them running home or to their car.

- Put a four-leaf clover on the front door made of green construction paper or purchase one that reads "Happy St. Patrick's Day" or "Luck of the Irish to Ye."

- Place a "Blarney Stone" near your front door. As guests enter your home, explain to them that it is an Irish myth that if you kiss the Blarney Stone, all of your dreams will come true. Tell them that if they kiss it, all of their wishes will come true. Find any ordinary medium sized rock, clean it, and, if desired, paint the words, "Blarney Stone" on it.

- Fill a witches cauldron or kettle left over from Halloween with gold foil-wrapped chocolate coins. Give one coin to each guest as they kiss the "Blarney Stone," or use the pot to distribute the candy for prizes.

- Make pictures of rainbows with pots of gold underneath one side of each rainbow, and hang in the party room. Cut out green four-leaf clover shapes and yellow horseshoe shapes and hang them in the party area.

- Hang maps or brochures of Ireland. Give them away as party favors.

- St. Patrick's Day tableware can usually be found right after Valentine's Day. If not, purchase a green tablecloth and use yellow tableware.

- Place a pot of shamrocks on the center of the table. These can be found in many floral departments of stores near the St. Patrick's Day holiday. Place toy snakes at the base of the pots. Another centerpiece idea is to place a vase of green carnations on the table. Give one to each guest as a party favor.

- You will need green shamrock stickers to place on anyone's shirt who did not come dressed in green. This should ward off any pinchers!

- Play lively Irish folk music near the front door as guests arrive to get them in the spirit of the party.

🎉 FOOD 🎉

- Ham
- Potato salad
- Potato bread
- Green Jell-O

  -or-

- Beef stew
- Potato bread

  -or-

- Corned beef and cabbage
- New potatoes
- Irish soda bread

With all of the above suggestions, serve:

- Green colored beverages: green Kool-Aid or green mint milkshakes (use vanilla ice cream, milk, peppermint extract and green food coloring)
- Serve rainbow sherbet, green lime sherbet, or green mint chocolate chip ice cream

Shamrock Cake

This recipe is a little different than most of the cake recipes in this book, in that it requires two boxes of cake mix. It also requires two one-layer heart-shaped cake pans. There will be a lot of cake, but I'm sure that you won't have any trouble finding volunteers to eat it!

You will need:

Two boxes of cake mix, plus ingredients as box directs
6 cups of white frosting
Green food coloring
Assorted candies: jellybeans, hearts (such as the kind left over from Valentine's Day), red string licorice

What to do:

1. Mix the first cake mix. Pour half of the cake batter in one heart-shaped cake pan and pour the other half of the batter in another. Bake and cool as instructed. Repeat with second cake mix.
2. When all cakes are completely cooled, place three heart cakes on a 20 × 24-inch foil covered board, like a shamrock. Cut a stem shape from the fourth heart cake. Cut it at the point, so that the point will fit in at the bottom of the shamrock. Let your family eat the remaining cake pieces that you no longer need.
3. Color all of the frosting green. Use a frosting bag fitted with a star tip to frost green stars all over the cake. Keep the stars close together, so that there are no gaps in between them.
4. Use the candy pieces to create a face on top of the shamrock cake. Use jellybeans for the eyes, a pink heart shaped candy for the nose and a strip of red licorice for the mouth.

Rainbow Cake

You will need:

1 baked 9 × 13-inch cake
5 cups of white frosting
Food coloring: red, yellow, blue and green
One 16-oz. can of chocolate frosting (you will only need about 1 cup of this)
Gold foil-wrapped chocolate coins

What to do:

1. Bake and cool cake as directed. Cut the cake as illustration shows (fig. 12a). If desired, freeze the cake pieces uncovered for about 1 hour to make the frosting spread easier.
2. Remove cake from freezer and arrange on a 15 × 20-inch foil-

covered board as shown (fig. 12b).

3. Color 2 cups of frosting red. Color 1 cup each of the following colors: yellow, blue and green.

4. Make the green grass using a frosting bag fitted with a small round tip. Pipe the frosting in swirls to appear as grass below the pot of gold.

5. Frost the outer edge of the rainbow red, the center yellow and the inner edge blue.

6. Frost the top half of the pot yellow and the bottom half chocolate. If desired, frost an edge at the top of the pot, using a frosting bag fitted with a rose tip. Frost a band of 3 layers to make it stand out well. Place the gold foil-wrapped candies on top of the pot, pushing them into the yellow icing.

☘ CRAFTS ☘

Makeup

When the children arrive, ask their parents' permission to paint green shamrocks or rainbows on their face with non-toxic face paint. Non-toxic face paint can be purchased at craft supply stores, or you can make your own by following the recipe below. Paint the girls' nails green. Finish off the look by sticking a green shamrock sticker on each child's shirt.

Caution: Before applying any makeup be sure that the children don't have any skin allergies, eye infections or cold sores. Never apply makeup under such circumstances.

Face Paint Recipe

You will need (for each color):

Plastic cup
½ tsp. Water
½ tsp. Cold cream

(a)

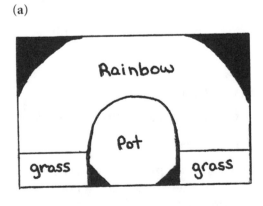

(b)

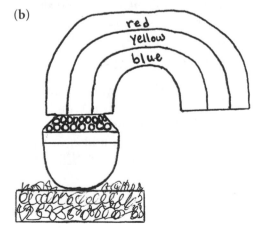

Fig. 12. Rainbow Cake

1 tsp. Cornstarch

2 drops of food coloring

What to do:

In a cup, mix the water, cold cream, cornstarch, and two drops of food coloring. Make several cups of the different colors that you need.

Whittling

You will need:

Inexpensive bars of green soap, 1 per child

Plastic knives, 1 per child

Newspaper

What to do:

1. Lay several sheets of newspaper out on a table or floor to protect the area from soap shavings.

2. Give each child a bar of soap and a plastic knife. Let them carve a shape out of the bar. Make sure that they carve the soap over a newspaper. Some ideas for shapes are shamrocks, animals, houses, cars, flowers, etc.

Green Carnations

On St. Patrick's Day, many people wear green carnations pinned on their shirt lapel. Purchase some to give to your guests. If you can't find any at a flower shop, make your own before the day of the party.

You will need:

A bucket or a large vase, filled with about 2 inches of water

White carnations, 1 per guest

Pruning shears or scissors

A few teaspoons of green food coloring or green ink

What to do:

1. Add the green food coloring or ink to the bucket or vase of water.

2. Cut the bottom of the flower stems at an angle, leaving the stem long enough so that the flower itself is out of the water.

3. Put the flowers in the bucket or vase. Place in a warm room. The flowers will turn green as the water travels up the stem to the flower, staining them green. This will take about 1 to 2 days. In 1 day the leaf edges will be covered. In 2 days the flower will be completely covered. If you have a sleepover this would be a great science experiment for the children. Do the experiment the night before and let the children wake up to find that their flowers have turned green.

Four Leaf Clover Good Luck Charms

You will need:

A shamrock plant (found at flower shops or stores that sell flowers and plants)

Clear laminate (the type used for protecting pictures and usually found near office supplies or the wallets department)

A large book, such as a phone book

What to do:

1. A couple of days or more before the party, snip the shamrock tops from their stems. Snip one for each guest. Place them under a heavy book to flatten for one day. Remove the shamrock and allow it to dry for another day.

2. During the party, ask the guests to choose a "four leaf clover." Give them some laminate paper and let them cut it to the size that they like, but at least ¾-inch larger than the clover itself on all sides.

3. Remove the paper backing and stick the shamrock on the sticky side. Cover with another piece of laminate, placing the sticky sides facing together. Press down removing any air pockets. Cut off excess laminate or adhesive. The children can cut the laminate in the shape of a square, circle, oval, heart, etc. If they are old enough to have a wallet, tell them to keep it in their wallets for good luck.

♟ GAMES AND ♟ ACTIVITIES

Potato Relay

You will need:

2 potatoes

2 tablespoons

What to do:

1. Divide the children into two equal groups and line them up behind a starting line.

2. Set a goal about 20–30 feet away from the starting line.

3. Hand the first child in each line a spoon and a potato.

4. On a signal to go, the first player in each line places the potato on top of the tablespoon and races with it to the goal and back. If he drops the potato, he must pick it back up and continue from that spot.

5. He passes the potato to the next child in line who then races as the first. The game continues in this manner. The first team to have each member complete the task finish wins.

Pot of Gold Treasure Hunt

You will need:

Gold foil-covered chocolate coins or gold plastic coins (use plastic if the weather is warm)

Cellophane or plastic lunch bags

Green gift wrap ribbon

A black pot (a witch's cauldron left over from Halloween works great or use an empty plastic margarine container painted black)

What to do:

1. Before the party, wrap the gold coins in individual bags or squares of cellophane and tie with a green ribbon. Put about 6 coins in each wrapper. Put some "gold" into the pot.

2. Just before or during the party, hide all of the coins, setting a few aside for any child who may not find many. Hide the pot of gold very well. If hiding the coins during the party, have another adult take the children into a front yard for another game, or a group picture at this time, so that the children are unaware of the second adult hiding the "gold."

3. The second adult comes into the front yard and says that he just saw a leprechaun running through the backyard with a pot of gold. He makes up a tall tale of how he saw the leprechaun drop some of his gold as he was running, and how he hid his pot and left. Then he tells the children to go and search for the gold. The child who finds the pot of gold wins a prize and shares the coins in the pot with everyone. The child who finds the most bundles of coins also wins a prize.

Note: Though it is rare, some very young children may be afraid of leprechauns.

Green List

Hand each child a pencil and a piece of paper. Tell the children to look around the house and list anything that they see that is green. Confine them to only the areas of the house that you want them to go. Tell them to consider everything, books on the bookshelf, scenes in pictures hanging on the wall, rugs, the curtains, wallpaper, etc. The child who returns with the longest correct list wins.

Irish Singing Contest

You will need:

Song sheets of Irish songs such as "When Irish Eyes Are Smiling" or "Danny Boy"

A recording of the songs chosen, optional

What to do:

1. Divide the children into different groups or allow the children to choose their own groups. It doesn't matter how many children are in a group, as long as there are at least two groups.

2. Allow the children to go into different areas of the home or yard to practice singing together. If any of the children are unfamiliar with the songs that you have chosen, an adult can play a recording of the song for them to hear or the adult may sing the song.

3. When they have had enough time to practice, allow the groups to take turns singing for the other groups. The best

sounding group wins — even if their version of the song is silly.

Kiss the Blarney Stone Relay

You will need:

2 small stones or rocks (see Decorations)

What to do:

1. Mark a starting goal and place the rocks 20–30 feet away from it. Divide the children into two equal teams and have them stand behind the starting goal.

2. At the signal to go, the first two children in line walk quickly to the stone, get down on their knees, kiss the "Blarney Stone," run back to the starting goal and tag the hand of the next person in line.

3. The next child in line does the same. This continues until one team has all of their members finish first. They are the winning team.

Four Leaf Clover Hunt

Three leaf clovers will abound, but a prize will be given when a four-leaf is found!

You will need:

Green paper

Three leaf clover stencils or a clover shaped cookie cutter (or use computer printed clover pictures)

Scissors

What to do:

1. Before the party, trace or print many three-leaf clover shapes, and draw one four-leaf clover shape. Cut them out.

2. During the party, hide the shapes around your home or yard. At a signal to go, send all of the children searching for the clovers. Award a prize to the one who finds the four-leaf clover, and award a prize to the child who finds the most three-leaf clovers.

Hot Potato

You may want to tell the children how important the potato is to the Irish people. The Irish are very dependent on potato crops. From 1845 to 1847, the potato crops in Ireland were struck with a disease (the potato blight) that devastated Ireland.

You will need:

1 potato
Celtic music

What to do:

1. Seat all of the children in a circle on the ground or floor. Hand the potato to one of the children.

2. At the start of the music, the children pass the potato around the circle clockwise.

3. When the music stops, the child caught with the potato is out of the game.

4. The music begins and the potato continues being passed.

This goes on until two children are left. The child who does not get stuck with the potato is the winner.

Note: So that the children who become out of the game don't feel left out or disappointed, you may consider letting each one control the music for one round, right after they are out. You could also give them a piece of candy as they become out, but give the winner something special.

Circle Blarney

Blarney is the Irish word for flattery. This is a Celtic dance.

You will need:

Celtic music (you can find Celtic music at many music stores or check with your local library)

What to do:

1. The girls form a circle in the center and the boys form a circle around them.
2. When the music begins, the girls march around in a counter-clockwise direction. The boys all march in a clockwise direction. If you don't have equal amounts of boys and girls, let some go in the other circle, if they like.
3. When the music stops, the boy and girl in front of one another

must "blarney" until the music starts again. They can dance around joined together at the elbows, or just stand there and flatter each other with insincere compliments until the music begins again. When the music begins, all march again.

Horseshoes

Purchase a set of horseshoes, found at many toy stores, and play a game of it. The horseshoe is a symbol of good luck and is associated with St. Patrick's Day. When hung upside down, like a "U" shape, it is said to catch good luck.

⚖ FAVOR AND ⚖ PRIZE IDEAS

Rubber snakes, items with shamrocks, leprechauns and rainbows on them (e.g., lapel pins, pencils, stickers, erasers, etc.), green derby hats, plastic gold coins, gold foil-wrapped chocolate coins, green jellybeans, maps or brochures of Ireland, bubble pipes, travel size boxes of Lucky Charms cereal or green peppermint candies.

Easter Party

• *Easter Sunday between* •
March 22 and April 25

Easter is the Christian festival that is celebrated around the world. The festival commemorates the resurrection of Christ. On Good Friday the ancient Romans put Jesus on the cross to die, and Christians believe that Jesus rose from the dead on Easter Sunday. The holiday is held on the first Sunday after the full moon on or after March 21. It is the most important holy day in the year for Christians. For many, the day is spent by first opening the baskets of goodies left by the Easter Bunny, going to church dressed in their Sunday best, eating a large feast with close family, watching the Easter parade and having a good old fashioned Easter egg hunt.

Easter is associated with symbols such as eggs and bunnies, because they are symbols of new life and the resurrection of Jesus. Since Jesus is believed to have died and come to life again, just as the plants come back and ani-

mals are born in the springtime, these symbols really do seem to be perfectly fitting for such a holiday. One of the reasons that Christians paint the Easter eggs is because, according to legend, when Mary Magdalene went to the tomb of Jesus, she took some hard-boiled eggs to eat. When she saw the risen Christ, the eggs were miraculously painted in rainbow colors.

The word "Easter" comes from the name "Eastre" or "Eostre" who was once believed to be the goddess of light and spring. Since Easter occurs during springtime, this is another reason many of the customs celebrated are based on the flowering of plants and the birth of animals that occur during this season.

In America, the Easter Bunny became a symbol of Easter after the Civil War. The custom was brought to the United States by German immigrants in the eighteenth century. The story of the egg-laying Easter Bunny comes from an ancient Anglo-Saxon legend. Eostre, the ancient goddess of light and spring, was said to have turned her pet bird into a hare, yet despite its new form the animal continued to lay eggs in its nest. The hare soon became a symbol of the Spring Feast and later, in the eighth century, became a symbol of the Christian holiday Easter.

Having a party based on the Easter theme is a lot of fun. Most children love a good Easter egg hunt. Even those who do not celebrate Easter will enjoy this party. Invite all of your child's friends over for some egg dyeing and fun games, and your party will be hoppin'!

🎉 EGG OR 🎉 BUNNY INVITATION

Use a cookie cutter or a stencil to trace the shape of an egg or a rabbit onto yellow paper, then cut out the shape and write your message as illustrated (fig. 13a & b). If using the egg invitation, decorate the front of the invitation with colorful designs made of paper. If using the bunny invitation, draw a bunny face on the front with eyes, nose, whiskers and a mouth. You could even use a small pink or red pompom for the nose. Cut pink oval shapes for the insides of the ears, and glue them on the front.

Another invitation idea would be to print an Easter picture with a computer. Write the birthday message shown. If you will be having an Easter

(a)

(b)

Fig. 13. Egg & Bunny Invitation

egg hunt, you may want to ask your guests to bring a basket to carry their eggs.

⚘ HELPFUL TIPS ⚘

- Do not plan the party too close to Easter Sunday. Many people leave town at this time to visit relatives or go on vacation. Others may be busy planning for an Easter celebration at their home.

- It is important for you to remember that if you don't know all of your child's friends, or your neighbors, there is a possibility that an invited guest may not celebrate Easter. If the invited guest or parent brings up this subject, explain to them that you won't bring religion into the party theme, and that their child is very welcome to participate in all of the activities anyway. This happened to me once, and the parent had the child bring a basket to participate in the egg hunt. The child really ended up having a great time. That was over five years ago and her mother says that her daughter still talks about how much fun she had that day.

⚘ DECORATIONS ⚘

- Hang pastel colored balloons and crepe paper from the mailbox, front porch and in the party area.
- Purchase or make a yard sign that reads, "Bunny Crossing."
- Purchase or make a sign for your front door that reads, "Happy Easter," or make a bunny out of paper.

- Hang plastic Easter eggs from tree branches by enclosing string in the egg.
- Make Easter eggs out of construction paper. Let your child decorate them with crayons, felt tip markers or paint. Hang them all over the house.
- Put an Easter lily at the front door. They smell great. If you have allergies, put it outside on the front porch, otherwise you may be sneezing during the entire party.
- Put stuffed animals such as bunnies, chicks and lambs in the party area.
- Decorate the table with an Easter tablecloth and tableware, or use green, yellow, purple and pink.
- For a centerpiece, you could use a stuffed bunny or an Easter basket filled with Easter grass and colored eggs. If you like, place plastic Easter eggs in the basket with a surprise inside. Tuck one end of a long ribbon inside of the egg. Close the egg tightly. Place the other end of the ribbon on each child's plate. Ask them to pull the ribbon at the signal to go. Each child may open his egg and see his surprise. Some eggs are made better than others, so check to be sure that they will stay closed during the pull. If they won't stay closed, tie a knot at the end of ribbon that goes in the egg before closing, and tape the egg closed with just a tiny piece of tape.
- Use plastic eggs as place cards with each child's name painted on them. You can also write the children's names on hard-boiled eggs with a crayon before dyeing it. The crayon will not take the dye, but the rest of the eggshell will. Another placecard

idea is to make egg shaped cookies and pipe the children's names on them with frosting. Allow the icing to set, then cover each with cellophane.

- Ask a friend or relative to come dressed in an Easter Bunny costume and hop around for the children. This person could pass out Easter eggs from a basket. Have your camera ready!

- Play a tape of the song or story "Little Bunny Foo Foo" or "Here Comes Peter Cottontail" (for children 6 and under).

🎉 FOOD 🎉

For a close family gathering, I am sure that your family already has its own wonderful menu traditions that are served every Easter. Ask each family member to bring a dish that they enjoy making and eating. The following menu suggestion would be for an event such as a neighborhood block party, church gathering or a child's birthday party. Party trays with such a menu can be purchased at many restaurants and grocery stores.

- Chicken nuggets: serve with a variety of sauces for dipping such as honey mustard, catsup, sweet and sour sauce, barbecue, and some children may even like ranch dressing.

- Carrot and celery sticks with ranch dressing for dipping

- Deviled eggs

Bunny Cake

You will need:

Two 8- or 9-inch round baked cakes
5 cups white frosting
Red food coloring
Yellow food coloring, optional
Jellybeans
Red string licorice

What to do:

1. Bake and cool the cake as directed. Cut cake as shown in the illustration (fig. 14a). If desired, freeze uncovered for about one hour to make frosting spread easier.

2. Remove from freezer and arrange on a 15 × 18-inch foil-covered board as illustration shows (fig. 14b).

3. For a bright looking cake, frost 4 cups of the frosting yellow, or you may choose to leave the frosting white. Use a star tip and a frosting bag to frost the white or yellow frosting on the cake. Frost all of the cake, except the center of the ears and the center of the bow.

4. Tint the remaining 1 cup of frosting pink, using the red food coloring. Frost the inside of the ears and bow with pink frosting, using the star tip.

5. Use the jellybeans for the eyes and nose. Use the licorice to make a mouth and whiskers as shown in illustration (fig. 14b).

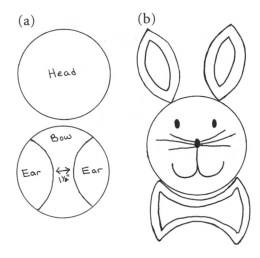

Fig. 14. Bunny Cake

Easter Basket Cake

You will need:

One round, baked two-layer cake
3–4 cups of white frosting
Food coloring: green and yellow
15 × ¾-inch piece of cardboard
Cellophane
Assorted candies: jellybeans, chocolate eggs, gummy bears, etc.

What to do:

1. Bake and cool the cake according to directions.

2. Color ⅔ of the frosting with yellow food coloring. Frost the top of one round cake with the yellow frosting and place the other round cake on top of it. Frost the sides and top edge of the cake yellow. If you are in a real creative mood and know how to do a basket weave design with frosting, go for it. But the cake will look good even if you don't use the basket weave design.

3. Color the remaining ⅓ of the frosting with green food coloring. Frost swirls of green frosting on top of the cake to resemble Easter grass, using a frosting bag fitted with a small round frosting tip.

4. Cover the 15 × ¾-inch piece of cardboard with cellophane. Bend it into a "U," creating the "basket handle" shape and push it into the top of the cake about 1 inch from the sides. Frost the handle yellow.

5. Place jellybeans, chocolate eggs and gummy bears onto the top of the cake, to appear as Easter basket filler.

Easy Easter Basket Cupcakes

If time is short, bake some cupcakes. For a special surprise, stick an unwrapped chocolate Easter egg into the batter of each cup before baking. Cool, and then frost the cupcakes with green tinted frosting, and use a frosting bag fitted with a small round tip to pipe swirls of frosting all over the cupcakes. These swirls will resemble green grass. Your child may enjoy helping you do this. It is very simple and fun for a child to do. Stick a few jellybeans and gummy bears in the "grass." Use a piece of licorice twist to make the Easter basket handle. Bend the licorice over into a "U" shape and push it into the frosting.

Easter Bunny Cupcakes

After mixing the batter for the cupcakes, stick an unwrapped chocolate Easter egg into the batter of each cup before baking. Bake the cupcakes, cool, and frost them yellow. To create the ears, cut an oval shaped cookie in half and frost it yellow. If desired, frost the center of the cookies pink. Stick the cookie into the cupcake as ears for the bunny. Use chocolate chips or small round candies for the eyes and nose. Cut string licorice for the whiskers and mouth.

🎉 CRAFTS 🎉

Candy Carrots

These "carrots" make great party favors at school, neighborhood or church events, or you could stuff them in some "bunny's" Easter basket.

You will need:

Rose colored plastic wrap
Yellow colored plastic wrap
Green colored plastic wrap
A clean, dry carrot
Jellybeans
Ribbon, optional

What to do:

1. Cut one square of rose and yellow plastic wrap. Place the rose colored wrap over the yellow colored wrap.

2. Place the carrot diagonally across the center of the wrap and fold the corner, at the point of the carrot, up to cover the end of the carrot. Roll the carrot in the plastic wrap.

3. Remove the carrot, creating a little pocket. Fill it ¾ full of jellybeans.

4. Wind green plastic wrap around the top to create a stem and tie with a ribbon.

Egg Dyeing

You will need:

2–3 hard-boiled eggs per guest
Newspaper
Egg dye
Non-toxic felt tip markers
Crayons
Empty egg cartons or cut paper towel rolls (for drying eggs)
A small amount of cooking oil
Plastic vegetable baskets (the type produce sometimes comes in), 1 per guest, optional
Easter grass, optional

What to do:

1. Cover the table or counter very well with the newspaper to protect it from stains. Prepare the dye in individual small bowls or cups, and set on top of the newspaper.

2. Have the children write their names and designs on their eggs with a crayon.

3. Let them dip their eggs into the dye. Help them if necessary. Place the eggs in an egg carton or cut paper towel rolls to dry. Play a game or two while the eggs dry.

4. When the eggs have dried, let the children decorate them with markers. Rub a drop of

cooking oil on each egg to give it a shine and set color. Set the eggs in a vegetable basket that has Easter grass in it.

Bunny Goody Bags

You will need:

Paper bags, 1 per guest

Precut yellow bunny ears, 2 per guest

Precut yellow bunny face shapes, 1 per guest

Precut yellow body shapes, 1 per guest

Precut pink insides of ears, 2 per guest

Cotton balls, 1 per guest

Craft wiggle eyes, 2 per guest, optional

Glue

Felt tip markers or crayons

What to do:

1. Before the party, place all of the items needed to make each bunny bag, except glue, markers and crayons, inside the bags. Place the bags on a table covered with a paper tablecloth or newspaper. Place a sample bunny bag on the table for the guests to look at.

2. As each guest arrives, have him assemble a bag by gluing on the precut pieces. The head will go on the bottom of the folded bag. The ears will go above the head at the bottom of the bag.

3. After a body piece has been glued to the front and back of

the bag, glue a "cottontail" to the backside of the bunny.

4. Let the children glue wiggle eyes on to the face and draw on the nose and mouth. This bag doubles as a puppet before the children use them for an egg hunt or a piñata.

Bunny Ears

You will need:

Plastic headbands, 1 per guest

Precut set of bunny ears made of white construction paper with cardboard glued to the back

Pink cotton balls

Glue

Stapler

What to do:

The children can make these during the party, or you can make them before. Glue the pink cotton to the insides of the ears. Attach the ears to the headband with a stapler by wrapping the construction paper around the headband.

Bunny Faces

Ask the children's parents if you may paint a bunny face on their child when they drop their child off. Use a cotton swab to put red lipstick on the nose. Use eyeliner for the whiskers.

Paper Baskets

See May Day Festival/Spring Party; Craft, Paper May Flower Basket.

🎩 GAMES AND 🎩 ACTIVITIES

The Bunny Hop

Now that everyone looks like a bunny play this activity.

You will need:

The music "Bunny Hop"

What to do:

1. As you begin playing the music, everyone places their hands on the shoulders or hips of the child in front of them.
2. Guests make two kicks out with their right foot. Then two kicks out with the left foot.
3. Hop forward. Hop backward. Hop forward again 3 times.
4. Then they clap once over their head. This continues until the song ends.

Jellybean Guess

You will need:

A jar
A bag of jellybeans
Pencils and paper, 1 of each per guest

What to do:

1. Before the party, count all of the jellybeans and write the amount on a small piece of paper. Fold the paper up, being sure to conceal the written number. Tape the paper to the bottom of the jar. Put all of the jellybeans inside of the jar, close tightly and put away until the day of the party.
2. During the party, hand everyone a slip of paper and a pencil. Tell the children to write down what they guess is the number of jellybeans in the jar, along with their name.
3. After everyone has had a chance to write down a number, remove the piece of paper concealing the correct number and show it to everyone. The one who guesses the closest number wins the jar of jellybeans. You may want to have an alternative prize handy for those who don't like jellybeans.

Pin the Tail on the Bunny

This is a game that can be used more than one time. It goes over well at school spring parties.

You will need:

A bunny shape cut out of felt material
A piece of posterboard
Fiberfill or cotton balls
Glue
Velcro
A blindfold: a scarf or a bandanna, and a clothespin for securing

What to do:

1. Before the party, glue the cotton balls or fiberfill to a rough piece of Velcro (the part that will best stick to the felt). These will appear as a bunny tails.

Glue the bunny shape to the posterboard.

2. During the party, have the children take turns trying to "pin" the tail on the bunny, while blindfolded. Gently spin the children around a few times to throw them off a bit, but stop them in front of the bunny. The child to get the tail the closest wins.

Easter Egg Hunt

If you have not instructed your guests to bring their own Easter basket, or you won't be making the Bunny Goody Bags, give the children a container of some sort to carry their Easter eggs in. A beach pail, inexpensive straw Easter basket, or even a small child's watering can all make for good Easter egg hunting.

You will need:

Plastic fillable Easter eggs, 5–8 per child

Large plastic fillable Easter eggs, 1 or 2

Glossy gold spray paint

Candy

Small toys or trinkets, optional

Nametags for each child's Easter basket, if they brought one

What to do:

1. Before the party, spray paint the large egg or eggs gold and allow to dry.

2. Open up all of the eggs and stuff them with candy and toys. Set in a good hiding place, so that your family won't be tempted to sneak the candy.

3. Before the party, or during the party while the children aren't around, hide all of the eggs around your yard. Set some aside for children who have trouble finding eggs.

4. As children arrive, put a nametag on their basket, so that no one get theirs mixed up with others.

5. On the signal to go, everyone races to find the eggs. If anyone has trouble finding enough eggs, bring out your reserved eggs. Sort of inconspicuously place eggs where they will see them. For smaller children, you may need to point the egg out to them. The child (or children) who finds the golden egg wins a prize, or the prizes inside of the egg may be prize enough. If you like, award a prize to the one who finds the most eggs, finds the most of one color, looked in the most places, etc.

Variation: Hide one egg for each guest with their name painted on it. Use larger eggs for these and put in a special note with goodies from your child. The note could say something like, "Erika, thank you for coming to my party. You are a great friend! I like the way you always make me laugh. Your friend, Jason." Tell the children not to pick up any egg that has someone else's name on it.

Bunny Hop Race

Have all of the children stand in a straight line along a stretched out string or a garden hose. At the signal to go, they must all hop like bunnies (standing or crouched low) to a finish line. Use another stretched out string or garden hose to mark the finish line. The first child to make it to the finish line is the winner.

Pass the Basket

You will need:

A basket

Stuffed plastic Easter eggs, 1 per guest

A big sucker or a large stuffed egg

Music (if you can find something with an Easter or spring theme that would be great)

What to do:

1. Put all of the eggs into the basket and seat all of the children in a circle. Hand the basket to one child.

2. Once the music begins, the children pass the basket around the circle clockwise.

3. When the music stops, the child stuck with the basket takes out one egg, keeps it, and leaves the circle. The great thing about this game is that he won't be concerned about being out, he will feel that he has won, because he will be off enjoying the goodies from inside of the egg.

4. Begin playing the music again and do as before, having one child leave the circle after the music stops. The last child left who doesn't get stuck with the basket wins the big sucker or the large stuffed egg and the last egg.

Egg Rolling Relay Race

Every Easter the president hosts the Annual Egg Roll on the White House lawn. The rolling of the giant egg represents the stone that was rolled away from Christ's tomb. Since you may not have a "giant" Easter egg, you may need to improvise a little. You can use large plastic eggs that can sometimes be found about 10 inches long. If you can't find something to resemble an egg, use ordinary balls or beach balls.

What to do:

1. Divide the children into 2 equal teams and stand them behind a marked starting line. Mark another goal line 20–30 feet away.

2. At the signal to go, the first child in each line "rolls" (no kicking) the egg or ball on the ground to the goal and back to the start, leaving the egg or ball on the ground for the next child in line.

3. The next child in line "rolls" the same as the first. This continues until one team has all of its player's finish first. That team is declared the winning team.

Egg Roll

Give each player a plastic or a real hard-boiled egg. Allow the children to compete against one another by rolling their eggs down a slanted board or a hill. The child whose egg gets down to the bottom first wins.

Balloon Hop Relay Race

Play just as you would the Egg Rolling Relay, only instead of rolling an egg or ball, the children must hop to the goal with a balloon in between their knees. Have extra balloons on hand. If someone's balloon pops, hand them another, but they must continue on from where the balloon pops. When they reach the goal, they may remove the balloon and run back to their team to pass the balloon off the next player.

Rabbit Relay Race

Play just as you would the Egg Rolling Relay, only instead of rolling the egg or ball, the children must hop to the goal and back with a stuffed bunny rabbit. Once they return to their team, they pass off the bunny to the next child in line. If they try to run instead of hop, they must start over, losing time for their team. Remind them this before the game begins, to ensure fairness.

Egg Relay Race

If you will be using real eggs, this game will be messy and should be played outdoors and at the *end* of the party. Since the real eggs may get on your guests' clothes as they fall, instruct guests to wear play clothes on the invitation. If using the real eggs, try to have a dozen or more on hand, just in case you should need them.

You will need:

Real uncooked eggs, hard-boiled eggs or plastic Easter eggs
Two spoons

What to do:

1. Divide the children into 2 equal teams and stand them behind a starting line. Hand the first two children in line an egg and a spoon. Place a goal 20–30 feet away from the starting line.

2. At the signal to go, the first child in line must place his egg on top of his spoon, run or walk as fast as he can to the goal, turn around and come back. If he drops the egg, he must pick it back up and replace it on the spoon before he may begin walking or running again. If you are using real eggs, and his egg cracks, he must get a new egg from an adult, who then passes it to him. The spoon must only be held by the handle.

3. When he returns to his team, he passes the egg and spoon to the next child in line who must do the same as the first child. This continues until the first team to have all of its members finish wins.

Egg Toss

This game is very messy, but a lot of fun! It should be played outdoors and at the *end* of the party. If using this game, it might be a good idea to instruct guests, on the invitation, to wear play clothes. If you want to keep everyone clean, use plastic eggs or hard-boiled eggs, but real eggs are so much fun!

You will need:

Real uncooked eggs, 1 for every 2
   guests
A whistle
A garden hose or a line of string

What to do:

1. Spread the hose or string out in
   a long straight line. Have the
   children choose a partner and
   stand along the stretched out
   garden hose or line of string.
   Line them up in two separate
   rows, facing their partners,
   with one partner on each side
   of the line. They should be
   about 3 feet apart.

2. Hand all of the children on the
   left side an egg. Remind them
   of how fragile they are!

3. Tell them when you blow the
   whistle, toss their eggs to their
   partners. Remind them to only
   toss it *once*. Blow the whistle
   and the children toss the eggs.
   Any two partners who break
   their egg are out of the game.
   They may want to go over to an
   outdoor water faucet to wash
   their hands afterwards.

4. When all of the children on the
   right have caught their unbro-
   ken egg, they take a step back.

5. The whistle is blown again, and
   all of the children on the right
   toss their egg back to their
   partners. This continues until
   only two children are left. They
   are the winners. If those two

partners wish, they can continue to toss the egg back and
forth to one another to see
which child wins among the
two of them.

Egg Throwing

Hang an Easter basket by the handle with a piece of rope. You can hang
it from a tree, basketball hoop, or even
a porch. Line the children up behind a
chair or a marked throwing line. As
you sway the basket like a swing, allow
them to each have a turn at tossing 5
plastic eggs into the basket. The child
to get the most eggs into the basket
wins.

Egg Piñata

See Holiday Piñatas.

🎉 FAVOR AND 🎉 PRIZE IDEAS

Chocolate bunnies, chocolate
eggs, jellybeans, blowing bubbles,
butterfly nets, small stuffed bunnies
or lambs, Easter theme items (pencils, pens, stickers, erasers, coloring
books, etc.), rubber balls, kites,
jump ropes, sidewalk chalk, Candy
Carrots (see Crafts), dyed hard-boiled
eggs (see Crafts), Bunny Ears (see
Crafts), or filled Easter eggs (see
Games and Activities, Easter Egg
Hunt).

International Children's Book Day Party/ National Dictionary Day Party

• *April 2 / October 16* •

International Children's Book Day (April 2) celebrates the birthday of Hans Christian Andersen, the famous Danish writer of children's fairy tales. National Dictionary Day (October 16) celebrates the birthday of Noah Webster, who wrote the first American dictionary. Celebrate one of these days by having a party at your child's school. Discuss ideas with your child's teacher and organize a classroom or grade-level party. Instruct all the children to come dressed as their favorite storybook character.

If your child is into reading, writing or listening to a great story, you may have just flipped to the best chapter for him. This can even be a great indoor party for a cold winter day or a hot summer day that just puts a damper on any type of an outdoor party. You don't need to be a bookworm to have a fun time at this party … read on and find out for yourself!

♠ BOOK ♠ INVITATIONS

If you really want to get your guests' curiosity going, make your invitations into miniature books. See below for instructions on how to make an invitation sure to grab any guests attention!

You will need:

Colorful pieces of construction paper cut 8 × 5¼ -inch, 1 per invitation

White typing paper for the inside pages cut 7½ × 4¾ inches, 4–5 pieces per invitation

A pen, typewriter or computer

A stapler

Glue

Envelopes 4⅜ × 5¾ if mailing

What to do:

1. Put all of the white pages together and fold them in half. Do not write anything on the outer piece of white paper, this will be glued onto the construction paper cover.

2. On the top of the first page write, "It's an International

Children's Book Day Party!" and below it write, "by" and your child's name, your name, or a teacher's name.

3. At the top of the next page write, "Acknowledgments." Below it write, "I would like to thank my parents (or whoever) for helping me plan an awesome party! It was a lot of fun and we had a ball getting ready for you to come!"

4. At the top of the next page write, "Contents" and below it write as follows:

	Page
Date, time, place	1
RSVP	2
Map (if necessary)	3

5. On the top of page 1, write the date, time, and place.

6. On the top of page 2, write, "Please call us at (list your phone #), by (add date). Your immediate response would be greatly appreciated."

7. On page 3 draw a map to your home.

8. On page 4 write, "We hope to see you at the party, because it just wouldn't be the same without you!"

9. At this time either photocopy the pages or print them on a computer.

10. Staple the pages closely along the fold and glue the outer pages to the inside of the cover (the construction paper).

11. Fold the cover in half and write, "It's an International

Children's Book Day Party!" on the cover with colorful ink.

🎉 DECORATIONS 🎉

- Decorate mailbox, front porch and party area with black, white and red balloons and crepe paper streamers.

- For the front door make a book-like decoration. Fold a large piece of construction paper in half. It should read on the cover, "Open this book for instructions to a fun time." On the inside pages write as the following examples show: "Party in progress"; "Quiet please, geniuses at work"; "Warning: kid zone beyond this door." On the last page write, "Knock 3 times here" and draw arrow below it pointing down to a large "X."

- Suspend pencils tied to string from the ceiling and give away as party favors.

- Make pretend book covers out of construction paper or printed on a computer. Give them crazy titles or write the names of your child's favorite books. Poke a hole in the top and suspend them from string.

- Use a white paper tablecloth and allow the children to write on it. Check with a paper supply store to see if they have very large sheets of paper that you can purchase for this. Use black and red tableware.

- For a centerpiece, stand well-known books on the table.

- For placecards, use small phone books with each child's name painted on theirs.

- Play songs like "You Can't Judge a Book by Its Cover" (Bo Diddley) or "Return to Sender" (Elvis Presley).

🎉 FOOD 🎉

Serve bread rolls, a platter of sliced luncheon meat and sliced cheese; let the children put their own sandwiches together. Offer some pickles and chips for side items.

Book Cake

You will need:

1 baked 9 × 13-inch cake

2 16-oz. cans of white frosting

Food coloring, of any color you choose

What to do:

1. Bake and cool the cake according to the directions. Cut the cake as the illustration shows (fig. 15) with a long sharp knife. Cut a line about halfway into the cake and down the center of the cake. About 2 inches from the center cut, trim the cake inward toward the center. You may cut a straight cut or a curve, the choice is yours. If you choose a straight cut, you can reserve the cut pieces and place them up on the ends to raise the

edges, if necessary. If the cake edges have fallen a little, this may be necessary.

2. Cut the outside edges of the cake at a 45-degree angle to form the slant of the pages.

3. At this point you may freeze the cake for about an hour to help the frosting spread easier.

4. Remove the cake from the freezer and frost the entire cake white. Pull a decorator's comb across the edges of the cake to give the appearance of pages. If you don't have a cake decorator's comb, you may use a fork as a substitute.

5. Color the remaining frosting in the color that you choose and put it in a decorator's bag fitted with a star tip. Frost a shell border around the lower edge of the cake. Change the tip to a No. 104 or a rose tip, and frost a bookmark. Add fringes to the bookmark using a No. 1 tip and write a message on the pages.

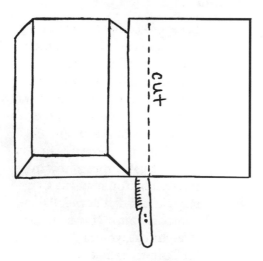

Fig. 15. Book Cake

Write something like, "Happy Birthday Lauren" on one page, and write "Chapter 12" on the other page. The chapter referring to the child's age and a new year or a new chapter in their life. Or the chapter could refer to the grade level of her class.

⚞ ARRIVAL ⚟ OF GUESTS

Book Discussion

As the guests arrive, let them get to know one another by just chatting for a few minutes while waiting on other guests to arrive. One good conversation starter would be to talk about some of the books that the children have read. They could do this while making bookmarks, or seat all of the children in a circle and have them take turns telling about the best books that they have read. Allow each child a set time to talk, then move on to the next child. Go in a clockwise direction. If that discussion goes well, ask the children to tell about the worst book that they have ever read.

Book Swap

Ask the guests on the invitation to bring an old or used book that they no longer want to "swap" with another guest. Everyone goes home with a new book to read!

CRAFTS

Bookmarks

You will need:

Colorful construction paper
Scissors
Felt tip markers
Clear laminate sheets or clear transparent contact paper
A hole puncher
Yarn

What to do:

1. Let the children cut the bookmarks out of the paper and design them any way that they like.

2. Cover the bookmarks with clear laminate sheets or clear transparent contact paper and trim excess.

3. Punch a hole through the top of the bookmark with a hole puncher.

4. Take a 12-inch a piece of yarn, fold it in half, thread the center of the yarn through the hole. Slip the other end of the yarn through the loop and pull it tight to secure the knot. If desired, make a fringe pompom by taking a few 4-inch pieces of yarn and laying them one on top of another. Tie them at the center with a small piece of yarn and knot it. Take the ends of the yarn on the bookmark and knot them to the string holding the pompom together.

You now have a book mark ready for a bookworm!

GAMES AND ACTIVITIES

Comic Strip Puzzles

Cut individual comic strips from the newspaper. Cut each strip into individual frames. Have the children put them in the correct order according to what they think should happen next.

Creative Writer Contest

You will need:

Typing Paper
Cardboard
Pencils, 1 per guest
Optional: crayons, felt tipped markers, stapler, cardboard, glue, ruler, fabric or wallpaper remnants

What to do:

1. Let the children lie on the floor or sit around a table; pass out some paper and pencils to them. Ask them to write the most creative story that they can think of. A short story will do. Give them about 20–30 minutes to write one. The story can be funny, scary, fantasy, science fiction, etc. Mention some ideas to them. Tell them to write a story about an alien who looks real scary, but turns out to be very friendly, or tell them to write a story about a

really mean teacher with buck teeth. You get the idea — make it fun, let them be goofy! As an incentive, tell them that the best story wins a great prize, and make sure that the prize is just that — something special. Show it to them to excite and motivate them!

2. If desired, lay out some supplies for the children to make their stories into books to take home. If doing this, fold several pieces of typing paper in half for the pages and staple them along the fold. Make these "book pages" before the party and let the children use them to write their stories on. Remind the children not to write on the first and last page, since it will be glued to the cover.

3. Cut the cardboard ¼-inch larger than the typing paper for a cover. Cover the cardboard with either fabric or wallpaper remnants for the book cover. Glue this onto the cardboard. Fold the book cover in half.

4. Glue the first and last page of the book to the book cover.

Note: The books can be assembled before the party to save time for other activities during the party. This would be a great activity for a slumber party, since you can take as long or as little time as necessary.

Newspaper Towers

This is a game that tests the thinking skills of the players. Each move must be carefully thought out before acting. Give the children plenty of flat open space to build their "towers."

You will need:

Several newspapers
Masking tape, about one roll per team, plus some for the pre-made rolls

What to do:

1. Before the party, roll the newspapers up, one large sheet at a time. Roll them tightly and secure with about three pieces of masking tape. You will need to make several of these newspaper sticks.

2. During the party, divide the children into two equal teams. Divide the sticks equally among two teams and give each a roll of masking tape.

3. Instruct each team on how to build a tower with their sticks and masking tape. The children all take turns adding to their group's tower. The first team whose tower falls loses. If neither fall, then the team with the tallest tower wins.

Variation: Give the teams 10 minutes. The team with the tallest tower when the time is up wins.

Crossword Puzzle Contest

You will need:

Photocopies of a crossword puzzle (possibly the subject of birthday parties, writing or book titles)
Pencils, 1 per guest

What to do:

Pass out the puzzles and pencils. At the signal, all of the children can begin. Give them about 10 minutes to get as much done as they can. The child who gets the most words correct wins a prize. An appropriate prize might be a crossword puzzle book.

Note: This contest may also be played with a word search puzzle. Make your own if you are unable to find one with the subjects that you are looking for.

Newspaper Dress Contest

You will need:

Several newspapers

Safety pins

Tape

Stapler, optional (this may be dangerous and is only recommended for older children)

Rubber bands

Directions on paper hat making (check your local library for a book on the subject)

Music

What to do:

1. Divide the children into groups. They must choose one child from their group to be the model.

2. Send them with their supplies into different rooms so that they may assemble the outfits on the model. Remind them to be careful not to accidentally stick the model with the pins or the staples. Tell them to be outlandish with their creations!

3. When everyone has finished, ask them to come out of the rooms.

4. Put on some music and have the models walk down a pretend runway and show off the creations. The most creative outfit from a group wins a prize for each member of the group.

Advertising Contest

You will need:

Plain white paper, 1 sheet per guest

Pens, pencils, crayons and markers

Rulers

An item to write about: a can of food, a box of cereal, a package of toilet paper, laundry detergent, a toy, etc.

What to do:

1. Give each child a piece of paper and other necessary supplies.

2. Show them the chosen item and tell them to write the most creative ad that they can think of for that item, or give each child a different item to write about. Remind them not to let anyone see their ads as they create them. Allow them to spread out around the room for privacy. Tell them that it is okay to be silly, if they like. For added fun, the ads can be spoofs on actual ads.

3. When all of the ads are finished, allow the children to read them one at a time. Let them hold and pitch their product, if desired. Applaud

each child as he finishes and encourage others to do the same.

4. Give a prize for the best ad.

Name the Product

This is a game best played by children old enough to understand popular advertising slogans.

You will need:

Magazines and newspapers
Photocopies or printouts of your list
Pens or pencils, 1 per guest
A timer

What to do:

1. Before the party, look through magazines and newspapers. Find about 15 popular or catchy slogans used by companies to advertise their products. For example, your list will look something like the following: "The best part of waking up is _____ in your cup" or "If it's got to be clean, it's got to be _____," etc. Photocopy your list or print it from a computer.

2. Give each child a list and a pen or pencil. Tell them to fill in the blanks. The one with the most correct answers within 10 minutes wins.

Book Relay

You will need:

Two hard-cover books, equal in size
Boundary markers

1. Divide the children into two equal groups and line them up behind a starting line. Mark a goal line about 15–20 feet away.

2. Hand the first child in each line a book.

3. At the signal to go, the first child in each line puts the book on his head, walks to the goal while balancing the book on his head, turns around and returns to the start. If the book falls, he must stop, put the book back on his head and continue walking.

4. He hands the book to the next child in line who then does the same. This continues until the first team has all of its team members finish the task first. They are the winning team.

Spelling Bee Contest

You will need:

Several 3 × 5-inch cards with different words written on them (make them age appropriate), 1 per guest
Pencil and paper, or a chalkboard to keep score on

What to do:

1. Put the cards together in a pile. Divide the children into two equal teams and stand them in a line single file. One team being team #1 the other being team #2.

2. Read the word on the top card to the first two children in line.

3. Give each a separate chance to

spell the word. Begin with the child on the left, then move to the child on the right. Anyone spelling the word correctly scores a point for their team. Give a tally mark to each team as their team member scores a point.

4. When the children have finished spelling the word, they go to the back of the line. When all of the words are used up, the team with the most points wins.

Note: A children's easel-type chalkboard works great for this game. The visual score makes the children more excited.

Silly Stories

Seat all of the children in a circle. One child or adult makes up two sentences of a story. Then the child to the left takes over, and adds two more sentences. The story continues on around the circle in a clockwise manner. The story can be about anything at all. Encourage the children to tell crazy, funny stories. End the story whenever you like, or when each child has had at least one turn. Let the last child tell the ending to the story, if you like. Get your video camera ready, you should get a kick out of watching this for years to come.

🎉 FAVOR AND 🎉 PRIZE IDEAS

Quill pens, fancy pens, pencils, felt tip markers, crayons, notebook pads, erasers, pencil bags, pencil sharpeners, miniature staplers, bookmarks (see Crafts), paint sets, phone books, word search or crossword puzzle books, inexpensive children's books, comic books, pocket sized dictionaries, thesauruses, diaries, journals, gummy worms, or a poem written about all of your child's friends (printed on pretty paper).

May Day Festival or Spring Party

• *May 1* •

Ahh ... spring is in the air, the birds are singing, flowers are blooming, trees are budding, and butterflies are flitting everywhere! The springtime is absolutely beautiful, isn't it? What a perfect time for a party outdoors. This party is sprinkled with fun springtime-theme crafts, activities and games. For a party that is a blooming success, dig no further!

☂ UMBRELLA ☂ INVITATION

Make an umbrella invitation as the one illustrated (fig. 16a & b) on brightly colored paper. Use a colorful felt tip marker to draw the lines on the front of the umbrella. Write your mes-

sage on the back as illustrated (fig. 16b), using a colored ballpoint pen. Maybe, if you're lucky, Mother Nature will lightly "sprinkle" a little rain on the day that you plan to hand-deliver your invitations. If it does rain, take your child to deliver them all decked out in a raincoat and boots, and carrying his umbrella. You may want to reconsider taking him out if the weather is too disagreeable. You wouldn't want him sick for his big day. Some other invitation ideas that you could use are: a flower shape ("Our house is bloomin' with fun surprises for you!"); a bird shape ("Fly on over to our house for some fun and games!"); a frog shape ("Hop on over to Jacob's house for a hoppin' good time!"); a turtle shape ("Race on over to Melissa's house for her birthday party!"). You can even print a spring theme invitation on a computer printer.

(a) (b)

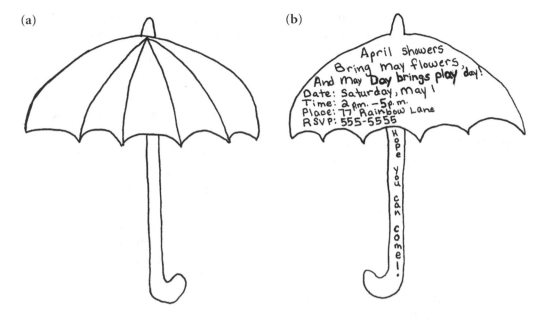

Fig. 16. Umbrella Invitation

🎉 DECORATIONS 🎉

• Decorate the mailbox, front porch, and party area with many different brightly colored balloons and crepe paper streamers. Hang the crepe paper so that it is free to blow in the breeze. It will look great.

• Make a brightly colored flower out of construction paper and hang it on the front door or gate to a fence. You could put a smiley face on the center of the flower, or write "Happy Birthday Jennifer!"

• Make colorful pictures of flowers, birds, umbrellas and green frogs out of construction paper or printed from your computer. Hang them around the party area.

• Make large flowers out of tissue paper and hang in the party area. To make them, place several squares of tissue paper on top of one another. Fold the tissue paper accordion-style and fold it in half. Staple at the end that has the fold and pull the layers apart. You now have a paper flower!

• Use a floral patterned tablecloth, or you could use a bright yellow colored tablecloth and have your child make brightly colored paper flowers in a contrasting color to tape to it. Use brightly colored tableware.

• For a centerpiece, put florist foam in a flowerpot. Stick green straws in the foam. (If you can't find green straws, paint some green). Make a flower shape, with petals, out of construction paper, and punch a round sucker, such as a Tootsie Pop, through the center of the flower. Place the sucker stick into the straw. Near the end of the party, give a sucker to each guest. Another centerpiece idea would be to place a vase of fresh flowers on the center of the table. If you have some growing in your yard, perhaps you could use them. Give a flower to each guest after the party.

- Play songs like "Raindrops Keep Falling on My Head" (B.J. Thomas), "Over the Rainbow" (Judy Garland), "You Are My Sunshine" (various artists), "Seasons Change" (Exposé), "Zip-a-Dee-Doo-Dah" (on the Official Album of Disneyland/Walt Disney World), "Fly, Robin Fly" (Silver Convention), "Free Bird" (Lynyrd Skynyrd), "Here Comes the Sun" (The Beatles), "Here Comes the Sun" (Richie Havens), "Itsy Bitsy Spider" or "The Garden Song" (Maria Muldar), "Little Birdie" (Pete Seeger), "Light Rain" (Shake Sugaree), "In My Garden" (Raffi), "Robin in the Rain" (Raffi), "Spring Flowers" (Raffi), "Magic Garden" (Craig 'n' Co.) or "Family Garden" (John McCutcheon). The latter nine songs are primarily for younger children.

🎉 FOOD 🎉

There are two vegetable choices given. One of the two should be plenty for small children. Since the flower fruit may take a few minutes to prepare, do this before the party and set in the refrigerator, or have a helper set the plates up for you during the party (not the person helping you with the children, you'll need him or her).

- Fried chicken legs (served hot or cold)
- Ants on a Log: Celery sticks filled with peanut butter or cream cheese and raisins or chocolate chips placed on top in a row to look like ants.
- Baby cut carrots or carrots with the green tops left on (wash and peel the carrot)
- Flower Fruit: Fan out orange slices or canned peach slices to look like flower petals and place a red maraschino cherry in the center.
- Bug juice: Use any green or yellow drink, and drop a gummy worm into each glass (tell the children to be careful not to swallow the gummy worm, and to chew it after the drink is gone).

Ice Cream

DIRT BUCKETS

These yummy ice cream surprises are sure to please any pint-sized fellow's tummy.

You will need:

Chocolate cookie crumbs, 2 tbsp. per cup, divided

Marshmallow creme topping, 2 oz. per cup

Chocolate ice cream, 2 scoops per cup

Chocolate syrup, 2 oz. per cup

Gummy worms, 3 per cup

Red licorice whips, 1 per cup

8-oz. clear cup or small buckets, 1 per guest

What to do:

1. Layer 1 tbsp. of cookie crumbs on the bottom of the cup or bucket.

2. Add a layer of marshmallow

creme on top of the cookie crumbs.

3. Add 2 scoops of ice cream.

4. Pour chocolate syrup over the ice cream.

5. Arrange gummy worms so that they extend over the edge of the cup or bucket.

6. Sprinkle 1 tbsp. of cookie crumbs on top.

7. Cut a 1-inch slit on each end of each licorice whip. Arrange the licorice to form the handle of the "bucket" by placing the cut slits over the lip of the cup or bucket. Serve immediately.

Note: If you would like to freeze these ahead of time, freeze them covered, and do not add the licorice or gummy worms until just before serving. Have another adult or a teenager prepare the finishing touches for you while you are entertaining your guests.

Butterfly Cake

You will need:

Cake mix for a two layer cake, plus ingredients as box directs

4 cups of yellow frosting

Assorted candies: gumdrops, M & M's candies and raisins

2 shish-kebob skewers or long pieces of uncooked spaghetti

What to do:

1. Mix the cake as directed. Pour a small amount of the batter into one cupcake liner set in a muffin pan, and divide the remaining batter among two greased and floured 8- or 9-

inch round cake pans. Bake the cupcake about 20–30 minutes and the cakes about 30–40 minutes, or until they test done with a toothpick. Cool as directed.

2. Cut each 8- or 9-inch round cake in half as illustrated (fig. 17a). Cut a small slice off the edge of each layer, on the rounded side, to create a flat side. Each layer becomes a wing to the butterfly.

(a)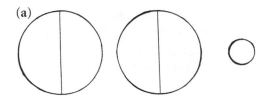

(b)

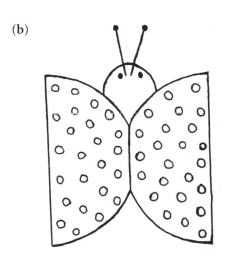

Fig. 17. Butterfly Cake

3. Freeze the cake pieces uncovered for about one hour to make the frosting spread easier.

4. Remove the cake pieces from the freezer. Place the layers with the flat part of the rounded sides together on a

foil-covered board of approximately 14 × 24 inches. Frost the top of each layer and place another cake layer on top of the first. See illustration for placement of pieces (fig. 17b).

5. Remove the paper liner from the cupcake. Trim and position the cupcake as the head.

6. Frost the entire cake yellow and top with sliced gumdrops, as polka dots, on the wings.

7. Make eyes with the M & M's.

8. Stick a raisin or gumdrop on the end of each shish-kebob skewers or uncooked spaghetti and position as the antennae.

Caterpillar Cake

You will need:

Baked cupcakes

5 cups light green frosting

Assorted candies: M & M's, large and small gumdrops (small gumdrops are optional)

1 green candy stick (green apple flavor or peppermint usually comes in green)

What to do:

1. Bake and cool the cupcakes according to package directions. Remove the paper liners.

2. Position the cupcakes as a curvy caterpillar on a large foil-covered board of approximately 15 × 24 inches. A large cutting board works great. See illustration (fig. 18).

3. Frost all of the cupcakes green.

4. Use two M & M's for the eyes. Use green gumdrops for the feet, which are placed all along each side of the cupcakes. Break the candy stick in half and position to resemble the antennae-like horns. If desired, slice colorful gumdrops and position as polka dots on the cupcakes. See illustration (fig. 18).

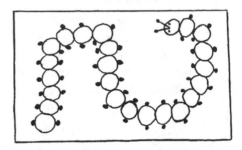

Fig. 18. Caterpillar Cake

Variation: If desired, crumble up some chocolate sandwich cookies with a rolling pin, to create "dirt" and lay it around the caterpillar. Place some gummy worms on top of the "dirt."

Bug Cupcakes

If time is short, frost baked cupcakes with green frosting and place plastic bugs on top of each cupcake. A party of boys should get a kick out these. To make lady bug cupcakes, frost cupcakes with white frosting and place one red-frosted vanilla wafer on top of each cupcake. Use brown frosting or black gel frosting to pipe polka dots on the red frosting. Pipe a line down the center of the red wafer. Frost a little brown or black head on the white frosting above the red frosted wafer.

CRAFTS

Paper May Flower Basket

It is an old tradition, still kept alive by some, for children to fill May baskets will flowers or goodies and to secretly deliver them on May 1 to friends and neighbors before breakfast. The children usually hang the baskets on doorknobs or set them on the front porch. Then, they ring the doorbell or knock on the door and try their darnedest to get away before anyone can detect them. If the basket recipient catches you they are entitled to a kiss — that is, if they should want one. This would be a great way to deliver your invitations! Simply staple the invitation to the basket of flowers or goodies, place the basket on the porch, ring the doorbell and run for your life!

You will need:

9 × 10-inch rectangles of colored
    construction paper, 1 per basket
Ruler
Pencil
Scissors
Brass paper fasteners, 2 per basket

What to do:

1. Cut off a 1 × 9-inch strip from the end of the paper rectangle as illustrated (fig. 19a). This strip will become the basket handle. The remaining 9 × 9-inch square will become the basket.

2. Divide the square into 3-inch sections by drawing lines on the paper as shown in the illustration (fig. 19a). The paper should have a 9-square grid drawn on it — like a tic-tac-toe grid.

(a)

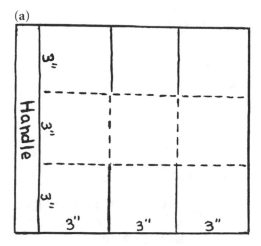

(b)

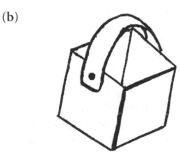

Fig. 19. May Flower Basket

3. Cut where the solid lines are shown in the illustration.

4. Fold where the dotted lines are shown in the illustration. You should now have a little box shape that is open at the top.

5. Attach the handle on each side of the basket with the paper fasteners, by pushing them through the handle and then through the three layers on the basket. Fold out the fasteners to secure handle. See illustration

(fig 19b). Your basket is now ready to be filled with spring flowers or goodies!

Flower Hair Wreaths

You will need:

Floral wire

Floral tape

Real flowers, artificial flowers, or tissue paper flowers

Wire cutters

Pliers

What to do:

1. Make a circle shape out of the wire, just big enough to set on each child's head.

2. Carefully twist the wire ends together so that no sharp points stick out. Cover any sharp points with plenty of floral tape.

3. Beginning at one end, and working your way around the crown, tightly tape the flower stems onto the wire. Place the flowers as close together as you can to hide the floral tape and any exposed wire. Completely cover the wire with flowers.

Decorated Flowerpots

Here are a few ways you may choose to decorate the flowerpots. The method that you choose will depend on the weather, the type of pot that you use and the length of the party. You can fill the pots with the flowers before the party and let the children paint the pots with the flowers in them, or let the children paint clay pots (which will dry quicker than plastic) at the beginning of the party and let them fill them with dirt and flowers at the end of the party. You can paint the pots yourself before the day of the party, allow them to dry, and let the children plant the flowers, or you can skip the plants and just let them paint the pots.

You will need:

Inexpensive clay or plastic flowerpots, 1 per guest

Newspaper

Acrylic paints in various colors

Disposable bowls or cups

Paint brushes, preferably 1 per guest

Can of clear gloss finish spray, optional

Plants such as pansies, marigolds, vincas, geraniums or petunias, optional

Bag of potting soil, optional

Small boxes, optional

What to do:

1. Before the party, write a child's name on the bottom of each pot with paint or permanent marker. Fill the pots with flowers, if you will not be spraying the pots with gloss or glaze, or painting the pots.

2. During the party, lay the newspaper out on a picnic table or on the ground. If using the paint, put the different colors of paint in individual bowls or cups and set on top of the newspaper with the paintbrushes. If possible, set up outdoors in the sun to help speed up the drying process.

3. Give each child the pot with their name on it to paint as they wish.

4. If you will not be planting flowers in the pot before or during the party, follow this step: Spray the pots with clear gloss finish as directed. Make sure that the wind isn't blowing and that there is no food or eating utensils around when you spray these. Also, have the children leave the area while you spray. Place the pots in a small box for the children to take home, or deliver them to the guests another day when they have dried, and with a note thanking your guests for attending the party.

Rock Paintings

This activity would be best performed outdoors, since it is messy. It could be started at the beginning of the party to allow enough time for drying.

You will need:

Smooth rocks, such as river rocks, 1–3 per guest
Newspaper
Acrylic paint
Disposable bowls or cups
Paint brushes, preferably 1 per guest
Can of clear gloss finish spray or a jar of clear drying glaze
Felt, optional
Glue, optional

What to do:

1. Before the day of the party, clean the rocks and lay out in the sun, allowing them to dry well.

2. During the party, lay the newspaper on a picnic table or on the ground. Set the rocks, paintbrushes and individual bowls of paint on top of the newspaper. If possible, set up outdoors in the sun to speed up the drying process.

3. Let the children pick out the rock or rocks that they would like and let them paint pictures on them. Some ideas to paint are flowers, ladybugs, butterflies, or smiley faces. Set aside, if necessary, to allow the rocks to dry before putting a finish on them.

4. Let the children paint over their designs with the glaze. If using spray gloss finish, follow step 4 of Decorated Flowerpots. Set aside in the sun to dry.

5. If the rocks have had a chance to dry, glue a piece of felt to the bottom of each rock. This will prevent the rocks from scratching desks or countertops. Suggest to the children that they use the rocks as paperweights, or save them to give to their parents for Mother's Day or Father's Day.

Bug Jars

You will need to begin saving jars for this craft well before the day of the party. Ask friends and relatives if they will save some for you. You could even ask each guest to bring one, but expect some to forget. Glass jars with metal lids work best for this craft. I have tried plastic jars, which would be perfect for this craft, but the hard plastic lids tend to crack when you hammer air holes in them. You can use a very fine drill bit to drill the holes in and it will work great, but the children won't be able to do this themselves. You will need to remind the children to walk, not run with the glass bug jars, since they can break. It would be best to use the jars in a yard.

You will need:

Clear glass jars with a metal screw top lid (cleaned and empty), 1 per guest
Hammer
Thin nail
Piece of scrap plywood, optional

What to do:

1. Hand each child a glass jar. Let them remove the lid and hammer the holes into the lid with the top of the lid against the plywood or over grass. An adult may need to help them hammer. Always hammer from the outside of the lid so that any sharp points will face inward toward the inside of the jar when the lid is in place. Hammer down any sharp points on the lid with the hammer.

2. Fill the bug jars with a little bit of grass clippings, twigs and leaves.

3. Send the children off into your yard to search for critters! Help them find some bugs by lifting logs from a woodpile, looking under landscaping or digging

in the ground. Remind the children to free the bugs either before they go home, or soon after they get home. It would be a good idea to teach them that it is great to observe bugs, but that it is important to leave the natural world as they find it. Each bug has its purpose, and many of them are good (e.g., pollinating the flowers or eating bad bugs). The bugs can't help us if they have croaked in a bug jar!

Leaf Rubbings

You will need:

Several different types of leaves
White paper
Crayons (old ones with the paper removed work best)

What to do:

1. Send the children out into your yard to search for leaves to collect. If you prefer not to have them pulling at your trees, collect them before the party begins.

2. Place the leaves on a flat surface, such as a picnic table and put the paper on top of it.

3. Rub a crayon over the paper sideways and see how the outline of the leaves and their veins appear.

Candy Carrots

See Easter Party.

Paper Flowers

See Cinco de Mayo/Mexican Fiesta Party.

🎩 GAMES AND 🎩 ACTIVITIES

Drop the Flower

You will need:

An artificial flower

What to do:

1. Have all of the children form a circle and choose one child to go outside of the circle.

2. Hand the child outside of the circle a flower. He must walk around the circle and drop the flower behind one of the children in the circle.

3. The one who the flower is dropped behind, must pick up the flower and chase the child who dropped the flower. He must catch him before he goes all the way around the circle and enters his spot that has been left vacant. If he catches the one who dropped the flower, the one who gets caught must go in the jail — that is, the center of the circle. If he is unsuccessful at catching the one who dropped the flower, then it is the one chasing who must go in the jail.

4. The game continues with the successor being the next one to

drop the flower. The only way to get out of jail is to grab the flower from behind someone where it has been dropped, before that person gets it. End this game whenever you like, or when there are so many children in the jail that the game can't continue.

Variation: Instead of having the child who is unsuccessful in catching the child to drop the flower go in the center, have him be the next child who has to drop the flower. Also, years ago this game was played to the song, "A-Tisket, A-Tasket." If you happen to have the song, play it for young children while playing this game.

Leap Frog Race

You will need:

2 long pieces of string or garden hose

What to do:

1. Tell the children to all choose a partner; if one child is left without a partner, play the game twice, so that he may have a turn. Try to make sure that partners are equal in size.

2. One partner gets down on all fours and squats like a frog. All of the squatting partners must be in a long straight line. Use a long stretched out garden hose or string to mark the start line and another to mark a finish line. It would be best to set this game up in a soft grassy area.

3. The other partner must stand behind his squatting partner.

At the signal to go, the partner standing in back must jump over his partner, by placing his hands on his partners back and jumping over him with his legs to the side.

4. Now, the partner that was in back squats down on all fours and the second player jumps over him. This continues until the first two partners to reach the designated winning spot. Those two partners win. An appropriate prize would be a toy frog for each.

Flowerpot Toss

You will need:

5 empty flowerpots, numbered 1–5 with paper labels
3 tennis balls or small rubber balls
List of guests' names
Pencil

What to do:

1. Arrange one pot behind the other, in numerical order, pot #1 being in front, #2 behind it, and so on.

2. Line the children up and give each 3 tosses at the pots. When a ball lands in a pot, the number on the pot is the score given. Add the total score and write it down next to the child's name. The child with the highest score wins. A ball would be an appropriate prize for this game.

Flower Hunt

You will need:

Silk or paper flowers (you can make flowers just as described under Decorations, but use facial tissues)
Something to carry the flowers in: beach pails, baskets, or even paper bags with flower stickers on them

What to do:

1. Hide the flowers all over your house or yard, before the party or while the children aren't around.

2. Hand the children the chosen item to carry the flowers in. At the signal to go, all race to find the flowers. The child who finds the most wins a bouquet of flowers or a packet of flower seeds.

Seed Guessing

You will need:

A variety of different seeds such as: apple, corn, bean, watermelon, orange, marigold, sunflower, etc.
Paper plates, numbered
Pencil and paper, 1 each per guest

What to do:

1. Place a different type of seed on each paper plate. If setting up outdoors, secure the plates so that they do not blow away. It may be necessary to tape the underside of the plate to the table with masking tape, or hold the plates down with rocks.

2. Hand each child a pencil and a piece of paper. They are to number their paper according to how many different types of seeds there are, and write down the name of the seed that they think corresponds with the number. The one to list the most correct wins. An appropriate prize would be a packet of seeds.

Variation: Do the same as above, but use leaves instead of seeds. Tape the leaves to the plate.

Ring Around the Rosebush

You will need:

A flowerpot with an artificial rose bush in it
1–3 hula hoops

What to do:

1. Mark a throw line on the ground and place the flowerpot about 8 feet away.
2. Have all of the children stand in line behind the throw line. Allow each child 3 tosses of the hula hoop to try and ring the flowerpot. Any child to ring the flowerpot wins a prize. If the hula hoop bounces off, it doesn't count. An appropriate prize would be a single stemmed rose.

Umbrella Penny Toss

You will need:

An umbrella
Pennies, 5 per child
Paper and pencil

What to do:

1. Open up an umbrella and turn it upside down, facing toward the children. Mark a throwing line 10–15 feet away from the umbrella. The distance will depend on the age of the children and the size of the umbrella.
2. Line the children up behind the throwing line and hand each child 5 pennies to toss into the umbrella. The penny must stay inside of the umbrella to count. Make sure that no one is in the way of the tossed pennies. After each child takes a turn, write down their score. The child to toss the most into the umbrella wins. An appropriate prize would be an inexpensive children's umbrella.

Jump Rope Contest

You will need:

Jump rope
Paper and pencil to keep score

What to do:

Give each child a turn at jumping the rope. The one to jump the most times without missing wins.

Jump the Rope

You will need:

Jump rope or a rope about 8 feet long

What to do:

Stand all of the children in a circle. Choose one child to stand in the center. The child in the center swings the rope around on the ground, and the other children must jump over it. Allow each child a 30 second to 1 minute turn in the center, depending on the age and amount of children in the group.

Maypole Dance

The Maypole dance is a folk dance of ancient origin. It is traditionally performed on May 1 as part of the May Day festival. The original origin of the Maypole itself is thought to have come from come from the Celts of prehistoric Britain, where large cone shaped mounds were built for the Maypole. One such hill is called Silbury Hill in Wiltshire, England. According to archeologists, the hill is at least four thousand years old. A pine Maypole was set on top of the hill, which was flattened at the top. The pole cast shadows down on the hillside and onto the level plain to the north, so as to mark the four seasons of the year. Determining the spring and autumn equinoxes was a very important factor in determining the correct planting times of crops. This could make a difference between famine and plenty. The building of these huge mounds and Maypoles would affect generations to come, and they were very important to the citizens. In England throughout the Middle Ages and the Renaissance, the Maypole was set up on May Day. The Puritans banned its use in 1644. The custom was later revived.

Some archeologists believe that the custom of the Maypole was introduced to the Egyptians by the Celts. It is possible that from there the pole calendar was spread to Italy, where the traditional Maypole dance originated. When the Romans settled in England and other parts of Europe, they brought with them their traditions of the Roman festival Floralia, which was held in April. The festival was to honor Flora, the goddess of flowers and spring. The Romans believed that the goddess would help their crops and animals grow. They gathered flowers to honor Flora and decorated their homes inside and out. The young girls would wash their faces in the morning dew from the flowers, which was said to restore youth. They would make flower wreaths for their hair (see Craft, Flower Hair Wreaths) and wear costumes with bells sewn onto them.

Eventually, Floralia was combined with the Celtic celebration called Beltane, which was held on May 1. The Celts of Beltane believed that the fairies were especially active at this time. In Medieval times, May Day became the favorite holiday of many English villages. People gathered flowers to decorate their homes and churches. They sang spring carols and received gifts in return. A May King and Queen were chosen for the festival. Villagers danced around the Maypole, holding the ends of ribbons that streamed from its top. They wove ribbons around the pole until it was covered with bright colors. The dance was performed to welcome the longer daylight hours.

Have a Maypole dance to welcome spring at your party. You will need something to resemble a Maypole. Tie crepe paper streamers to the top of it and bring them down to the ground. If you have a basketball pole at your home that may work. Another idea is to decorate a cardboard wrapping paper tube and stick it in the umbrella hole of a picnic table. If you like, have the children tie bells to their shoelaces like the traditional folk dancers do.

To begin the dance, have the players stand in two circles. If you have equal numbers of girls and boys, place the girls in the inner circle facing clockwise. Place the boys in the outer circle facing counter-clockwise. The dancers all grab the end of a crepe paper streamer. When the music begins, they skip around the pole in opposite directions. First the boys go over the girl's heads with their streamers and the girls wind their streamers under the boys. They keep winding until the streamers are completely wound around the pole. They then reverse the dance and unwind the streamers. To unwind the streamers, the girls form an outside circle and the boy go in the inner circle. This time the girls raise the streamers over the boy's heads.

Wheelbarrow Race

See Independence Day/Fourth of July Party.

☝ FAVOR AND ☝ PRIZE IDEAS

Seed packets, gummy worms, beach pails, play shovels, play rakes, watering cans, real flowers, pinwheels, sidewalk chalk, jump ropes, rubber balls, plastic toy bugs, bird whistles, paper or silk flowers, kites, butterfly nets, inexpensive umbrellas, Paper May Flower Baskets (see Crafts), Flower Hair Wreaths (see Crafts), Bug Jars (see Crafts), Painted Rocks (see Crafts) or Decorated Flower Pots (see Crafts).

Cinco de Mayo Festival or Mexican Fiesta

• *May 5* •

In Mexico, the word fiesta means party or feast, and much of the colorful tradition of the fiesta comes from the ancient Mayans. The Mexicans love a fiesta and find any excuse to have one! The big enchilada of all of the fiestas is Cinco de Mayo (May 5). Gather all of your friends and neighbors together and plan an exciting block party with this theme. If your child's birthday is near this time, why not consider a Cinco de Mayo party? Of course your child's birthday doesn't have to be anywhere near the month of May to have an exciting Mexican fiesta party. Any time of the year is a great time for one. Most Mexican fiestas usually include a piñata for the children, and are almost always at children's birthday parties. If your child is big piñata fan this is definitely the party to have one at. Let your imagination run poco loco and create a miniature Mexican vacation that will bring your child and guests south of the border for a fun party the Mexican way!

🎉 FIESTA 🎉 INVITATION

Make an invitation as the one illustrated (fig. 20a & b) on bright, colorful paper. Write your message on the front and the inside as illustrated. Use a hole puncher to cut out little confetti circles in several contrasting colors and glue them on to the front of the invitation. If you will be hand-delivering the invitations, you can attach some colorful strands of curled paper ribbon to the invitation. Another idea for a fiesta invitation is to make your invitation in the shape of a Mexican sombrero. You can also print an invitation from a computer. Put a festive looking picture on the front of the invitation and put little pictures of Earth, Mexican flags, confetti or firecrackers on the inside of the invitation.

(a)

(b)

Fig. 20. Fiesta Invitation

🎉 DECORATIONS 🎉

- Hang very colorful balloons and crepe paper streamers from the mailbox, front porch and in the party area.

- Put a sign on the front door that reads "Hola! It's fiesta time amigos" (Hello! It's party time friends!) or "Hola!—Bienvenidos a mi casa!" (Hello! Welcome to my house!).

- Hang colorful lights on trees, bushes or from porches for nighttime parties.

- Hang colorful paper chains from the ceiling and over the front door.

- Buy or make pictures of cactus, sombreros, donkeys, bulls, maracas, Spanish dancers or the Aztec sun god. Many party supply stores have a great selection of fiesta decorations.

- Hang a Mexican flag or make one out of paper. The colors are divided into equal thirds. First green, then white in the center, and last red. The colors stand for earth, purity and blood. The center of the flag has a bird holding a snake in its beak.

- Hang a map of Mexico.

- Write signs that say "Fiesta amigo," "Happy fiesta!" or "Bienvenido" and hang in the party area.

- Make a banner that reads "Felíz Cumpleaños!" (Happy Birthday!) and hang it in the birthday area.

- Use red, white and green for the tablecloth and tableware or purchase Mexican fiesta tableware.

- Hang a piñata or use one as a table centerpiece. Buy a piñata or see Holiday Piñata chapter to learn how to make one yourself. You could also use a sombrero or a vase of bright paper flowers as a centerpiece.

- Arrange to have someone play the traditional Mexican birthday song "Las Mañanitas" on a guitar, or play lively Spanish music such as "La Bamba" (Los Lobos) or "Mexican Handclapping Song" (Ella Jenkins). My personal favorite recording of Spanish music is a children's recording called "Fiesta Musical: A Musical Adventure Through Latin America for Children" with Emilio Delgado ("Luis" of *Sesame Street*). The children at my daughter's birthday party, ranging in ages from 3 to 12 years old, loved the music. Even the adults couldn't help but dance to it. The children especially liked the song "La Acamaya" (Eugene Rodriguez & Artemio Posadas Jimenez).

🎉 FOOD 🎉

Tortillas are the national bread of Mexico. Corn tortillas have been the basis of Mexican food since 10,000 B.C.

Serve some sort of filled tortillas. Corn or flour tortillas can be used as a wrap for almost any food.

The Aztecs of Mexico were the first to make chocolate from the cacao tree found in Mexico, so you may also want to serve something made of chocolate. Tell the children that we should be very thankful for the discovery of chocolate from the ancient Aztecs.

- Tacos: Put the meat and topping ingredients in separate bowls and allow guests to assemble their tacos the way that they like. Have toppers such as shredded lettuce, shredded cheddar cheese, chopped tomatoes, sliced olives, chopped onions, mild salsa and sour cream.

- Tortilla chips with mild salsa.

- Serve Choco Tacos ice cream with the cake.

Fiesta Cake

Decorate a baked sheetcake with any color frosting you like and pipe on the word "¡FIESTA!" with frosting or you can write it on the cake with string licorice. Pipe a shell border on the cake with a star tip and decorate the cake with candy confetti or sprinkles. If desired, make curled streamers out of chewy fruit roll snacks. Cut each fruit roll strip into several long thin strips using a clean straight-edge razor. Roll each strip around the handle of a wooden spoon and store covered at room temperature for about 8 hours. Once the curl is set, remove from the handle and place the streamers on the cake.

Señorita Doll Cake

Make the skirt a bright color such as yellow or red. You could even place a male Mexican doll on a doll stand next to the female doll cake.

You will need:

2 quart, half round, oven-proof batter bowl

1 box of cake mix, plus ingredients as box directs

3–4 cups of white icing

Food coloring

Doll pick (found at craft and kitchen supply stores)

Cake decorating flowers (found at grocery stores, on the baking aisle), optional

What to do:

1. Preheat oven to 350° F. Prepare cake batter according to package directions and pour into a greased and floured batter bowl. Bake 55–65 minutes or until tested done when a cake tester or a wooden skewer inserted in the center comes out clean.

2. Cool for 15 minutes on a cooling rack. Invert on a serving platter or a foil-covered board. Cool cake for 3–4 hours before decorating.

3. Insert the doll pick into the top of the cake.

4. Color the frosting in a bright color with the food coloring. Frost the entire cake.

5. Use a frosting bag fitted with a rose tip to make flowing ribbons across the cake or "skirt."

6. Make flowers to put on top of the ribbons, using the rose tip. If you don't know how to make frosting roses, buy store-bought cake decorating flowers.

7. Finish off the dress by decorating a frosting bodice on the doll body, using a frosting bag fitted with a small star tip.

🎉 CRAFTS 🎉

Paper Flowers

Colorful tissue paper flowers can be seen hanging in the streets of Mexico during fiestas. They are sold on the street corners. Make some to decorate your home or as a party craft.

You will need:

Tissue paper in assorted colors and cut in squares approximately 5 × 5 inches

Pipe cleaners

Scissors

What to do:

1. Cut out different sizes and colors of tissue paper as illustrated (fig. 21a).

2. Layer the tissue paper, putting large pieces on the outside and smaller pieces on the inside.

3. Punch two holes in the center of each set of tissue paper layers.

4. Put a pipe cleaner through one hole, bend it, and put it through the other hole as illustrated (fig. 21b). Make sure that

the two ends are even. Twist the two ends together to make a stem.

Variation: To make large paper flowers, use large sheets of tissue paper. Place several squares on top of one another. Fold the tissue paper accordion-style and fold in half. Staple at the end that has the fold and pull the layers apart.

(a)

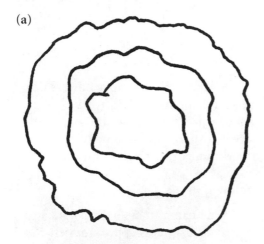

(b)

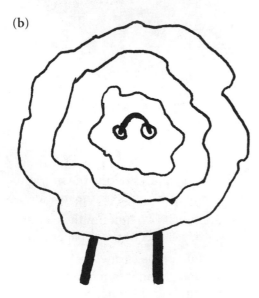

Fig. 21. Paper Flowers

Maracas

You will need:

Foam drinking cups, 2 per maraca
Dried beans, very tiny pebbles or rice
Masking tape
Aluminum foil
Colored construction paper
Glue
Scissors

What to do:

1. Fill one cup with a small handful of dried beans, pebbles or rice.

2. Tape the two cups together, at the lip of the cups.

3. Wrap the cups with aluminum foil.

4. Let the children cut designs out of the construction paper and glue them onto the aluminum foil. Shake, shake, shake, and you have a pretty maraca ready for a fiesta dance!

God's Eyes

In South America, children are given God's Eyes on their birthdays. Each different color of wool stands for a year of the child's life.

In Spanish these are called Ojo de Dios. Translated in English that means the Eye of God. They are also known as Magic Eyes or String Crosses. Some believe that the Incas were the first to make these, while others believe that it was the Pueblo Indians. The Mexican Indians are famous for their beautiful handmade fabrics. The weaving styles of the God's Eye differs throughout

Mexico. It is possible to identify an Indians regional homeland by the colors and patterns that they use. These crosses are very easy to make, once you get the hang of it. Practice before the day of the party, so that you will be able to show the children and your helpers how to make them. You will need to have a lot of help from other adults or teens for this craft, otherwise it will be too chaotic. Depending on the age of the children, expect to have about 1 adult to every 3–4 children.

You will need:

Yarn remnants of various colors, preferably bright colors
Thin wooden sticks, twigs, popsicle sticks or even straws
Scissors
Wooden beads, optional

What to do:

1. Tie two sticks together at their centers, forming a cross as illustrated (fig 22a). Wrap the yarn evenly once or twice around each stick. Knot the ends of the yarn tightly, so that it will not come undone in the center.

2. Continue around the cross in a clockwise manner wrapping the string first *over* each stick, then wrap the string around the stick going *under* the stick. See illustration (fig 22b). Bring the string back *up* and move on to the next stick in the same manner. Push close to the center so that there are no gaps, but not so close that it appears all bunched up.

3. After you have gone around the circle a few times in one color, cut the string and tie on another color string. Clip off the excess string from the knot as close to the knot as you possibly can. Continue on around the circle with the new color as before. Change colors as often as you like to give a unique and colorful design. For an interesting look, use 3–5 different colors. Tie a knot to finish.

4. If desired, glue wooden beads or string tassels onto the ends of each stick after the God's Eye is complete.

5. Make a hanging string and tell the children to hang these decorations from their bedroom doors. See illustration (fig. 22c).

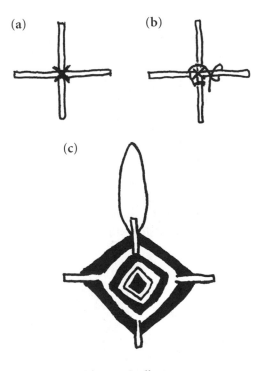

(a)   (b)   (c)

Fig. 22. God's Eyes

Walnut Castanets

You will need:

Walnuts
Small nail
Hammer
Strong thread

What to do:

1. Open up a walnut and empty out the meat inside.

2. Using the hammer and nail, tap a small hole in the upper end of each shell.

3. Tie the shells together with the thread. You now have a set of castanets ready to make music!

To play: Hold the castanets in your hand, and bending your palm together, click the shells.

GAMES AND ACTIVITIES

Teach Some Spanish Language

Before the party, teach your child how to say a few of the following examples and you will have your guests speaking it too! It's fun!

English	Spanish
Hello	Hola (OH-la)
Please	Por favor (pour-fah-VOHR)
Thank you	Gracias (GRAH-see-ahs)
Thank you very much!	¡Muchas gracias! (MOOchass grah-see-ahs)
Boy friend	Amigo (ah-MEE-go)
Girl friend	Amiga (ah-MEE-gah)
Boy	Ñiño (NEE-nyo)
Girl	Ñiña (NEE-nya)
Goodbye my friend!	¡Adiós Amigos! (ahd-eeh-OHS ah-MEE-gos)
Until tomorrow!	¡Hasta Mañana! (AH-sta mah-NYAH-nah)

Mexican Hat Dance

If you plan on giving inexpensive straw sombreros as party favors to your guests, this is a great opening game to disperse the sombreros. This game is not the traditional Mexican Hat Dance known as Jarabe Tapatió, but it is just as fun to watch. The traditional Mexican Hat Dance features couples dressed in splendid outfits, who dance to the accompaniment of a mariachi band. The dance is a courtship dance in which sombreros are placed on the ground, danced around, and stepped on by the women. This action symbolizes a happy conclusion that the women have accepted the proposal of the men.

You will need:

Sombreros, 1 per guest
1 small ball, such as a tennis ball
Lively Mexican music ("La Acamaya" is perfect for this game)

What to do:

1. Put all of the sombreros in a circle on the floor or ground. Have all of the children stand in a circle around the sombreros.

2. Have all of the children turn their back to the sombreros and ask them to cover their eyes. While they are covering their

eyes, quietly place a ball under one of the sombreros.

3. Tell the children to uncover their eyes.

4. Begin playing the music and have the children dance with their hands behind their backs, somewhat like a Mexican Hat Dance, around the circle clockwise until the music stops.

5. When the music stops, everyone must stop in front of the hat nearest to their feet. Then all of the children pick up the sombreros that they have stopped in front of. The child who stops in front of the sombrero with the ball under it gets to keep the sombrero, but is out of the game. He of course is so excited that he gets to keep the hat, that he doesn't care if he is out of he game. As far as he is concerned, he won!

6. Continue playing the music and playing in this manner until there is only one child left. This lucky child wins a prize, but all are winners of the hats!

Variation: Play this game with 2 balls, if you have a lot of children, and if you want the game to move fast.

Pin the Tail on the Donkey

This game can be purchased at many stores that sell party supplies, but if you can't find one, make your own as described below. You can even change the rules to something different like "Pin the Horns on the Bull" or "Pin the Mustache on my Amigo (Friend)."

You will need:

Brown construction paper

Black construction paper

Black markers

White crayon or liquid correction fluid

Tape

Blindfold: bandanna or scarf with a clothespin for ease in securing

What to do:

1. Before the party, cut a donkey shape out of brown construction paper. Draw on eyes, nose, mouth, hooves, etc.

2. Cut out one donkey tail for each child from the black construction paper. With white crayon or liquid correction fluid write each guests name on the front of a tail.

3. The day of the party, hang the donkey on a wall, door, refrigerator, tree or even a garage door.

4. Put a loop of tape on the back of each donkey tail. Line the children up single file and hand them their donkey tail.

5. Blindfold the first child in line and gently spin him around 3 times, ending with him facing towards the donkey.

6. He must then try to "pin" the tail on the donkey while blindfolded. Proceed with each child the same way. The child whose donkey tail comes closest to the spot where the tail belongs, wins.

Hat Toss

You will need:

1 sombrero
5 unshelled peanuts
Pencil and paper

What to do:

1. Place the hat on the floor or ground so that the opening of the hat faces up and toward where the children will be standing.

2. Allow each child to toss 5 un-shelled peanuts from behind a marked line that is set about 5–8 feet away from the hat. Write down each child's score after his turn. The child to get the most peanuts into the hat wins. An appropriate prize would be a bag of shelled peanuts.

Caution: Do not play this game with very young children. They may choke on the peanuts.

Aztec and Mayan Ruins

Tell the children that the Aztec and Mayan people were expert builders who constructed large pyramids, tem-ples and palaces in which they wor-shipped many gods.

You will need:

2 decks of cards or a lot of building blocks
A timer or a stopwatch

What to do:

1. Divide the guests into 2 equal teams — one team being the Aztecs, the other being the Mayans. If you have a lot of children, add another team.

2. Hand an equal amount of cards or blocks to each team. Tell the children that they are to work together to build the tallest pyramid. If using cards, have the children build their towers on carpeting. A table will be too slippery. Blocks can be used on any level surface, as long as there is plenty of room.

3. Give each team 5 minutes to build their pyramid. The tallest one built in 5 minutes wins.

Peanut Pitch

The Aztecs played a game called Patolli on a board in the form of a cross. They used beans for dice, hence the name of the game — Patolli are beans in Aztec. The game described below is different from the way the Aztecs played Patolli, but somewhat similar.

You will need:

5 unshelled peanuts
Chalk or masking tape
Pencil and paper

What to do:

1. Before the party, make a large "X" on the ground as illus-trated (fig. 23), using either the masking tape or chalk, or both. Make 9 squares in the shape of an "X." Mark the center square 10 points, the remaining squares 5 points each, and the triangles 1 point each.

2. During the party, line the children up behind a marked throwing line that is about 5–8 feet away from the playing square. Allow the children to takes turns tossing the 5 peanuts, all at one time, onto the square playing area. Add up their score after they toss, and record it on paper next to their name. The child with the highest score wins a prize. A packet of bean seeds would be an appropriate prize.

Caution: Do not play this game with very young children. They may choke on the peanuts.

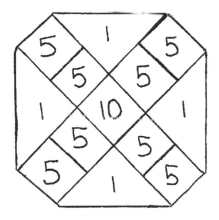

Fig. 23. Peanut Pitch

Disc Toss

The Mexicans play a game called Cuatro, or Four, which requires holes in the ground. Discs from 3 to 4 inches in diameter and 1 inch thick are thrown at the holes, which are just large enough for the disc to fit in. A disc falling into the hole counts as 4 points and one near it counts a 1 point. For a different version of this game see below.

You will need:

1 flying disc
1 hula hoop

What to do:

1. Set the hula hoop on the ground and mark a throwing line about 15 feet away.

2. Line the children up behind the marked line and give each child a throw of the flying disc. Anyone getting the disc inside of the hula hoop or closest to it wins a prize.

Variation: Attach the hula hoop to the top of a pole that is hammered into the ground with tape or string. Stand the guests approximately 8–10 feet away and let them try to throw the flying disc through the hoop. Anyone successful wins a prize.

El Toro (The Bull)

Bullfighting was introduced to Mexico immediately after the Spanish Conquest and is still popular. The passes with the cape are imitated in various folk dances, and everywhere children play at bullfighting. The first bullfight in Mexico was on August 13, 1529, to celebrate the taking of the Aztec capital in 1521. Afterwards, bullfights became a feature of all celebrations.

You will need:

Red cloth or cape
Stopwatch or a second hand
Whistle or horn
Pencil and paper

What to do:

1. Line the children up behind a marked starting line. Have an adult stand with the cloth about 20–30 feet away from the starting line.

2. At the blow of the whistle or horn, the first child in line charges like a bull, with his hands held up to his head like two horns, toward the cloth or cape. At the moment that the whistle or horn is blown, an adult begins timing the charging "bull" with a stopwatch or second hand. As he runs, the "crowd" or other guests all yell "Toro, Toro, Toro…!"

3. When the child hits the cloth with his "horns," the stopwatch is stopped and the child's time is recorded. The next children in line each take a turn. The child with the quickest time wins. An appropriate prize would be a stuffed bull.

Huesitos

During the apricot season, the children in Mexico play a game called huesitos, or little bones, with apricot pits. A hole is dug into the ground just big enough to hold one pit. The children take turns at throwing their pit at the hole from a certain distance. The child whose stone falls into the hole wins all of the stones around it. If you like, play this game with large marbles. Award all of the marbles or a small prize to the winner.

Mexican Bingo

In Mexico, the game bingo is called La Lotería or lottery. The Mexican version of the game consists of having 9 pictures on each bingo card instead of numbers. The pictures are: a boat, a guitar, a flower, animals, a key, a ladder, dice, etc. Corn seeds or bean seeds are used as markers. The game is played just like our version, where you must get a straight line across either vertically, horizontally or diagonally. You can make your own cards by printing pictures such as these on a 9-square grid with a computer printer. Make each bingo card layout different from the others. Make cards that you can draw from a bowl to call out the pictures to be marked.

El Jarabe de la Botella (The Syrup of the Bottle)

The Jarabe is danced by a couple, each taking a turn at dancing over a bottle, while the other sings a warning not to throw it over, because if any of the liquid is spilled it will have to be filled again. As each person takes a turn at dancing over the bottle these are he words that are sung: "Come on, compadre, dance the bottle [the person dances over the bottle]. If you throw it over, you will return it full. Come on compadre, keep on dancing it. If you spill it you will refill it." Then another player dances over the bottle. These verses are repeated until the dancers tire. Then they both sing: "The cloud is dissolved, the storm is over, if you're tired why don't you sit down?" Play this game with a small water-filled plastic soda bottle. Let the players take turns hopping over the bottle to the words of the song. All observers join in singing as the player whose turn it is hops. Anyone who does not knock over the bottle may win a prize. A sweet piece of candy would be an appropriate prize.

Volcanic Sacrifice

You will need:

Bucket
10 unpopped popcorn kernels
Pencil and paper

What to do:

1. Place the bucket on the ground and mark a throwing line on the ground.

2. Give each child a turn at tossing the 10 unpopped popcorn kernels into the bucket from the throw line. After each child takes a turn, write down how many kernels they get into the bucket. The child to get the most in, wins a prize. An appropriate prize would be a box of caramel popcorn.

Cattle Roping

Cattle roping was first introduced to Mexico from Spain. The Spaniards taught their Indian slaves the skill. These ropers were called vaqueros who later taught American cowboys their skills.

You will need:

Something to resemble a bull with horns: a decorated bike, a box with a stick through it, etc.
Lariat: a rope with a hula hoop tied

to it; a rope with a sliding noose, etc.

What to do:

1. Decorate the "bull" before the party and set it up in the yard.

2. During the party, stand the children behind a marked throwing line about 10–15 feet from the bull.

3. Let them take turns throwing the rope and trying to lasso the bull's head. Give each child three tosses of the rope. The one to get the rope or hoop around the bull's head the most times wins.

Mexican Amigo Piñata

A Mexican Fiesta Party would not be complete without a piñata. Buy or make a piñata. See Holiday Piñata chapter to make one.

Bull or Ox Piñata

See Holiday Piñata chapter for directions on how to make this.

Hot Tamale

Play this game just as you would the game Hot Potato. Cut a red pepper shape out of cardboard, and glue on red construction paper as the pepper, and use green construction paper for the stem. See the St. Patrick's Party game Hot Potato for rules to this game.

🎉 FAVOR AND 🎉 PRIZE IDEAS

Paper Flowers (see Crafts), Maracas (see Crafts), castanets, God's Eyes (see Crafts), sombreros, packets of bean seeds or peanuts (see Peanut Pitch), small stuffed bulls, marbles, maps or travel brochures of Mexico, Mexican clay figurines or pottery, small leather change purses, Mexican beaded jewelry, Mexican pesos (currency), Mexican cigars (bubble gum cigars) or Hot Tamales cinnamon flavored candy.

Independence Day (Fourth of July) Party

• *July 4* •

The 4th of July is a perfect time for a party! Independence Day brings thoughts of the signing of the Declaration of Independence in 1776, the ringing of the Liberty Bell, American flags proudly flying in the neighborhood, incredible fireworks displays, cookouts with family and friends, fun lawn games and a day of good old-fashioned fun that leaves everyone feeling good. Gather your family together for a family reunion or plan a neighborhood block party in celebration of America's birthday. Read on for some party ideas that will have everyone in a happy patriotic mood!

🎉 AMERICAN 🎉 FLAG INVITATION

Cut a piece of white 8½ × 11-inch paper into 4 equal sections of 5½ × 4¼ inches each. Cut red construction paper stripes that are ⁵⁄₁₆ × 5½ inches each. Glue the stripes on the white paper to appear as the American flag. Begin at the top with a red stripe and end at the bottom with a red stripe. Cut a square out of blue construction paper that is 2½ × 2½ inches. Glue the square onto the top left corner of the flag. You can place star shaped stickers on the blue section. You may not be able to fit the correct number of stars, but it will still look good. Write a message on the back of the invitation that reads "Uncle Sam Wants YOU at the Shepherds' 4th of July party! Please come and join us for some good old-fashioned fun and games." Write the date, time, place and your phone number. If you like, ask your guests to bring a covered dish to share. Chances are that the 4th of July around your home is sweltering hot, so instruct guests with children to bring their swimsuits, towels and water guns. Let them run through the sprinkler or swim in a pool. Place the flag invitation in a $4\frac{3}{8} \times 5\frac{3}{4}$-inch envelope to mail it. Another invitation idea would be to print your invitation on computer printer paper that looks like an American flag and can usually be found in office supply stores. These preprinted flags work best when planning a large-scale event, since they can be printed quickly from a computer or a copy machine.

⚑ DECORATIONS ⚑

- Hang red, white and blue balloons and crepe paper streamers from the mailbox, front porch, fence and in the party area.

- Fly an American flag in front of your house and push small American flags in the ground along the walkway to the house.

- Make a flag out of red, white and blue construction paper and put silver star stickers over the blue section. Hang the flag on the front door, garage door or gate.

- Make or purchase a picture of the

Liberty Bell, complete with a crack.

- Make cardboard stars and cover them with aluminum foil. Punch a hole in the top of each and suspend them from ceilings, trees and porches with fishing line.

- Use a 4th of July theme tablecloth and tableware found in many stores near the 4th of July season. You could also use a blue tablecloth and make aluminum foil stars to tape to it. Use a cookie cutter to trace the star shapes onto the foil and then cut them out. Use red and white tableware.

- Use blue and red bandannas as placemats or napkins.

- Make or purchase an Uncle Sam hat and use it as a centerpiece. Hide surprises under it for the children. Cardboard Uncle Sam hats can be found in some party supply stores.

- Play John Philip Sousa's march music or other patriotic music, such as "God Bless America," "National Anthem," "Star Spangled Banner," "Stars and Stripes Forever," or "You're a Grand Old Flag."

- Have a few fireworks, but keep the children at a safe distance away from them. Follow the directions on the fireworks' labels. Buy your fireworks from a licensed dealer. Check your local fire codes to make sure that fireworks are legal and that there hasn't been a ban on them due to drought conditions. It is also important to keep them away from any flammable party decorations.

🎉 FOOD 🎉

Have a third or fourth helper at the party to help cook on the grill. Cook one of the following meats and have a variety of side dishes:

- Chicken, hamburgers or hot dogs served with condiments
- Chips
- Potato salad
- Corn on the cob
- Clear plastic cups of blueberries and strawberries with a dollop of whipped cream on top (the colors being red, white and blue look great!)
- Watermelon slices (see Games and Activities) or a Watermelon Basket (see below)
- Bomb Pops popsicles, or Red, White and Blue Sundaes: 1 small scoop of raspberry sherbet, 1 small scoop of vanilla ice cream, ¼ cup of blueberries, topped with whipped cream and a cherry. Yummy!

Watermelon Basket

You will need:

1 large oval shaped watermelon (if you can get an oval seedless one that would be great)
1 honeydew melon
1 cantaloupe melon
Strawberries, cleaned and hulled, optional

What to do:

1. Cut the watermelon to look like a basket as illustrated (fig. 24).

If you like, get creative and make a zigzag cut along the edge.

2. Scoop out the red part of the melon with a melon baller and place it in a large bowl. You should now have an empty watermelon rind shell.

3. Cut the honeydew and cantaloupe in half and remove the seeds. Use the melon baller on one-half of each of these melons also.

4. In a large bowl, gently mix half of the watermelon balls with the honeydew and cantaloupe balls, using a large plastic spoon.

5. Place the melon-ball mixture into the hollowed out watermelon rind basket.

6. If desired, place strawberries on top of the melon balls.

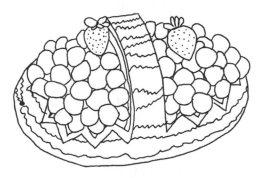

Fig. 24. Watermelon Basket

American Flag Cake

If you will be making this cake for a birthday celebration, use sparkler-type candles or trick candles. Serve the cake after dark, with the lights dimly lit for an interesting effect.

You will need:

1 baked 9 × 13-inch cake
3–4 cups of white frosting
Blue and yellow food coloring
2 cups fresh strawberries, cut into
    pieces
Toothpicks

What to do:

1. Bake and cool the cake as directed. Place the cake on a large foil-covered board.

2. Frost all but the upper left ⅓ corner of the cake white.

3. Color about ¼ cup of frosting yellow and set aside. Color the remaining frosting blue and frost the top corner of the cake. Pipe yellow stars on the blue square.

4. If desired, use any remaining blue frosting to pipe a blue border around the bottom edge of the cake and to pipe the "Happy Birthday" message on the foil-covered board.

5. Shortly before serving, have a helper place the strawberries on the top of the cake in seven rows to represent the red stripes of the flag. If you like, use a piece of string or dental floss to mark the lines. The top edge of the cake should begin with a red stripe and the bottom edge should end with one.

Variation: You can also use red frosting to pipe on the stripes.

ARRIVAL OF GUESTS

Make a goofy facsimile of the Declaration of Independence. Have someone with a great sense of humor write it. As each guest arrives, hand him a feather pen and ask him to sign his name to it.

CRAFTS

Fancy Fireworks

You will need:

Empty toilet paper tubes, 1 per guest
Colored tissue paper, optional
Colored construction paper
Scissors
Candy or small toys
Tape
Colored ribbon or string
Glue
Star stickers, optional

What to do:

1. Wrap a square of tissue paper or construction paper around an empty toilet paper roll. The tissue paper or construction paper should extend about 4 inches from each end. Secure the paper with tape.

2. Stuff the toilet paper tube with some candy and toys.

3. Tie a piece of ribbon or string around the paper on each end

of the tube to hold in the goodies.

4. Cut the extended paper into various strips to appear as sparks coming out of a firework. Fan out the strips.
5. Cut shapes out of construction paper and glue them onto the fireworks and stick on star stickers.

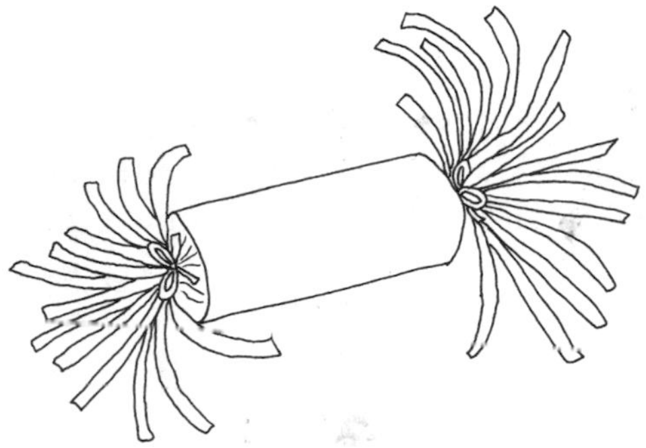

Fig. 25. Fancy Fireworks

Decorated Hats

Have the children decorate inexpensive hats or caps (found in craft stores). Put glue, plastic gems, beads and fabric paint on a table that is protected with newspaper. Let the children decorate their hats as they please. Plastic sunvisors can also be used for this craft.

Lightning Bug Safari

If you will be having an evening party, send the children outside after it gets dark to search for and collect lightning bugs. See May Day Festival/Spring Party, Craft, Bug Jars, to see how to make these.

GAMES AND ACTIVITIES

Independence Day Words

This is a good activity to do while waiting for other guests to arrive. Write the words Independence Day vertically on a sheet of paper (one sheet per child). Hand each child a sheet and a pencil as they arrive. See who can make the most words from the letters in Independence Day. See example:

I-nvention
N-ecklace
D-ark
E-xam
P-etunia
E-ntrance
N-ose
D-iver
E-lectricity
N-iece
C-olor
E-yeball

D-esert
A-irplane
Y-oung

Name the United States

Hand each child a piece of paper and a pencil and ask them to write down as many of the United States as they can think of. Give everyone about 10 minutes to finish. The one listing the most correct wins. An appropriate prize might be a laminated placemat of the United States or a puzzle of the United States with each state labeled.

Fourth of July Parade

If all of the children attending the party live around your neighborhood, ask them to decorate their bikes, tricycles, battery operated cars, wagons, go carts, or other riding toys before the party. Or if you like, you can provide the supplies for the children to decorate their bikes. You could provide items in the patriotic colors of red, white and blue, or use items that you already have around your home. Use crepe paper to weave in and out of bike spokes. Hang ribbons from handlebars and put balloons on the back of the bike seat. Have a parade to let everyone show off how hard they worked to make their bikes look good. Give anyone who does not have a toy to ride or pull, borrow one, or give them an instrument to play (e.g., flute, horn, whistle, kazoo). If you like, have a contest afterwards. Award a prize to the prettiest, funniest, craziest, best theme, most colorful, most unusual, most creative, etc. Make sure that everyone wins a prize.

Sack Race

You will need:

24-inch wide × 44-inch high burlap sacks (if you can't find any, sew some with burlap fabric)

What to do:

1. Divide the children up into two equal teams and line them up behind a starting line. Hand the first child in each line a sack to step inside of. Mark a goal line about 20 feet away from the starting line.

2. At the signal to begin, the first two children in line hop to the goal while holding onto the edges of the sack, turn around and hop back to their team.

They must always stay in the sack while hopping.

3. Once they return to their team, they get out of the sack and hand it to the next child in line, who must also get into the sack and do the same as the first child. The race continues on in this manner. The first team to have all of its members finish first wins.

Song Contest

Play a patriotic song for all of the children to hear. Then allow each child a turn at singing the song without the music. The one who gets the song the most correct or complete wins. You may also want to do this with a current popular song. You can also divide the children into groups and let them compete. When the guests sing as a group, they tend to be less embarrassed or shy about singing. But you may have a child or two who is quite a ham and has no problem with the complete, undivided attention given to him.

Three-Legged Race

Have each child choose one partner. Perhaps an adult can join any child without a partner. Line all of the children up along a stretched out garden hose or a line of string. Have the children stand next to their partners with their legs touching. Tie each set of partners together at the legs that touch with a strip of fabric or a rope. Tie them below the knee, but not too tightly, since it may hurt when they walk. At the signal to go, all partners race to the finish line, which is another long, stretched out garden hose or line of string. The two partners to make it to the finish line first wins.

Hit the Sucker

This game must be played outdoors, since it is messy. To play this game you must get a really brave volunteer who doesn't mind getting all wet. This volunteer may want to dress in a swimsuit. Many times an adult who is fun loving and very hot will gladly volunteer as your "sucker," just to cool off!

You will need:

Hula hoop or a large board with a hole cut in it (big enough for an adult's head to fit in and out of)

Filled water gun

Tub of water or a hose for refilling the water gun

Eye goggles

What to do:

1. Before the party, suspend the hula hoop from a tree branch or basketball pole, or prop the board up against a tree.

2. You must have a really brave volunteer and ask him to put the eye goggles on to protect his eyes. Have him stick his head through the center of the hula hoop or through the hole of he board.

3. Line the children up single file behind a marked line. Hand the first child in line the water gun. Allow 10 seconds to shoot the water gun at the "sucker." Anyone hitting the sucker wins ... a candy sucker!

Variation: This game may also be played with a *small* water soaked sponge.

Watermelon Seed-Spitting Contest

Now what would a 4th of July party be without a watermelon seed–spitting contest? It would be un–American! Line all of the children up and hand them each a slice of watermelon. Tell them to see who can spit the seeds the farthest. Have a hose handy for rinsing off afterwards.

Note: Make sure that you don't accidentally buy a seedless watermelon. Clean up the slippery seeds afterwards.

Ring the Liberty Bell Relay

You will need:

2 handbells

2 chairs

What to do:

1. Divide the children up into two equal teams and stand them behind a marked starting line. Place the chairs 20–30 feet away from the starting line and place a bell on top of each chair.

2. At the signal to go, the first child in each line races to his team's chair, rings the bell and returns to his team to tag the next child in line who then must do the same. The game continues on in this manner. The first team to have all of its team members finish first wins.

Tug of War

You will need:

Long nylon rope that is soft on the hands

Red bandanna or a piece of scrap material

2 sticks or pieces of string

What to do:

1. Fold the rope in half to determine where the center of the rope is. Tie the bandanna or piece of scrap material at the exact center of the rope.

2. Place the two sticks or pieces of string on the ground about 6 feet apart.

3. Divide the children up into two equal teams. To make the game fair, divide them up equally height and size wise. Place each team on opposite sides of the bandanna and tell the children to grab onto the rope as tight as they can. Make sure that the center of the rope is exactly in between the two sticks or pieces of string.

4. At the signal to go, tell the children to try to get the flag on their side by pulling the rope as hard as they can. The team to get the bandanna or piece of material across their stick or piece of string wins.

Pie-Eating Contest

You will need:

One small pie for each guest, or just fill aluminum pie plates with whipped cream

Picnic bench or table

Rope or string, a piece for each guest, optional

What to do:

1. Place the pies in a line along a bench or table. Have all of the children kneel down in front of the bench or stand in front of the table. Tie their hands behind their backs with the rope or string, since they can't use their hands for this contest, or you may tell them to keep their hands behind their backs.

2. At the signal to go, all dive in and start eating their pies. The first child to eat his entire pie wins. Have a camera ready to snap a picture of their faces; they will be quite a sight! Have a hose handy for them to rinse their faces after you snap the perfect picture.

Wheelbarrow Race

You will need:

2 garden hoses or a long pieces of string

What to do:

1. Set up this game over a soft surface, such as grass by marking a starting line with a long stretched out hose or string. Mark a finish line 20 feet away with another hose or string.

2. Have each child choose a partner, preferably someone their own size, and have them stand behind the starting line. One child is the "wheelbarrow," and

puts his hands on the ground behind the starting line, and his legs are held by the second player, who walks behind the "wheelbarrow."

3. At the signal to go, all sets of team members race to the finish line wheelbarrow style. The two partners to reach the finish line first win.

Variation: For a more challenging race, have the partners switch positions after they get to the finish line and then return to the starting line. The first two partners to return win.

Frog-Jumping Contest

If you live in a place where there is an abundance of frogs, catch two before the party. Feed the frogs well the night or morning before the party. They eat grubs, worms, flies, crickets and other insects. During the party, divide the children into two teams. Make a starting line and a finish line with string or garden hose. Place the frogs on the ground (not on the hot pavement), preferably on the grass. Have the children take turns pounding the ground "behind" their team's frog, to try and make the frog jump to the finish line. The team whose frog gets to the finish line first wins. Make sure that that the children are gentle with the frog. If the children and the frogs are manageable, allow each child a turn. The team whose frog wins or to score the most wins, is declared the winning team. An appropriate prize might be a plastic jumping frog for each member of the winning team. After the game, let the frogs go and have the children wash their hand very well with soap and water.

Variation: This game may also be played with turtles.

More Game Ideas

Play some traditional 4th of July favorites such as horseshoes, lawn darts, volleyball, bocce ball, croquet, badminton and Frisbee. Hand everyone a water gun and have a water gun fight. If you have a pool, let everyone take a dip in it. Provide sunblock for your guests and supervise everyone very closely near the water.

🎉 FAVOR AND 🎉 PRIZE IDEAS

Small American flags on sticks, items with flags on them (lapel pins, playing cards, pens, pencils, erasers, notepads, stickers, etc.) skimmer hats, water guns, pinwheels, sidewalk chalk, beach balls, suntan lotion, sunglasses, kites, ball and jacks sets, Fancy Fireworks (see Crafts), sunvisors (see Crafts), laminated placemats of the United States of America, suckers, or sacks of red, white and blue candy.

National Grandparents Day Party or Family Reunion

• *1st Sunday after Labor Day* •

National Grandparents Day is the ideal time to gather all of your family members for a family reunion that your children will remember for many years. You may even have some great memories of holiday celebrations with your own grandparents. If you never had a chance to get to know your grandparents, change that for your own children and start creating some good old-fashioned memories for them. With the ideas in this chapter, you'll have grandma and grandpa tickled pink!

⚐ INVITATIONS ⚐

Before planning a big bash and sending out invitations, check with the guest/guests of honor, especially if you are planning on making the party a combination of a birthday or anniversary celebration. Some people expect a big hoopla made when they reach a certain milestone in their lives, while others don't like parties at all, especially if they are the guests of honor. So before you even consider planning a big bash, find out what the guests of honor's wishes are. You may be surprised to find out that a small family get together is what would make them the happiest. It would also be a huge load off your shoulders to find this out before you plan a big party, instead of after it is over with. When printing the invitations, try to keep the age of the guests in mind. If many of the guests are elderly, print the invitations in large bold print to make them easy to read.

🎉 GIFT IDEAS 🎉

- Make a handwritten or computer-printed coupon book with coupons that read: "Coupon good for one snow shoveling, yard raking, back rub, housecleaning, grass cutting, errand to the grocery store, trip to the doctor, trip to the beauty salon, cooked dinner, planting in the garden, weeding of the flowerbed, etc." Elderly people are sure to appreciate this book! They may have all that they need around their home as far as gifts go, but one thing that they may always need is help around the house, and company. This is especially true for a widow or widower. For children or teens that want to give their grandparents a present, but don't have any money, this idea is perfect!

- Homemade cards from young grandchildren sometimes can mean more than the most expensive card in a card shop. Seat your children down with some crayons or felt tip markers, and tell them to draw the best card for grandma or grandpa that they can. It may be the one card that stands out from all of the prettiest "store-bought" cards received. My mom has her refrigerator in her basement covered with pictures from all of her grandchildren. It makes the grandchildren feel good to see those pictures hanging there. It shows them just how much she appreciates their artwork.

- If the guest of honor has difficulty seeing, purchase large print cards or reading material.

- If you know of a baked goodie that the guest/guests of honor likes, bake it for them and wrap it up with colored cellophane wrap and ribbons. Place it in a basket with a bow on the handle to give to them.

- Give a basket of fruit or a decorated tin of their favorite nuts.

- Gift certificates from the phone company are always appreciated. Many seniors love to talk to family, but are concerned about the cost of running up their phone bill. This will allow them to call you worry free. These also make great holiday gifts.

- If they love to garden, purchase some plants and offer to help plant and take care of them.

🎉 FOOD 🎉

In many parts of the country, the weather is fairly nice during National Grandparents Day, not too hot and not too cold. If the weather is nice in your area, plan an outdoor picnic. Ask everyone to bring a covered dish that they enjoy making.

Find out what the guest/guests of honor enjoys as a beverage. Many older people who once enjoyed beer, wine or liquor, may no longer be able to drink it due to a condition or medication. Their favorite drink may have changed from what you last remember them wanting. If this is the case, you might consider serving lemonade, iced tea, cider, sparkling grape juice, or sodas.

The same rules may apply to food as with beverages. Grandma or grandpa may have loved rich chocolate cake with frosting last year, but may no longer be able to eat it after a heart attack or a cholesterol test. Find out what their favorite meals are and serve one of them.

Dessert

Most seniors don't like a lot of frosting on their cake, so if you use it on a cake, go sparingly. Many older people prefer angel food cake, sponge cake, pound cake and pies. Check with them before making a dessert. If their absolute favorite dessert is blueberry pie, make it for them. Serve the dessert of choice with a candle in the center of it for a birthday celebration. There is no golden rule that states that the dessert *has* to be cake on a birthday or during other celebrations. Serve whatever makes them happy. Make or buy a small cake for those guests attending the party who would prefer cake.

🎉 THE PARTY 🎉 ATMOSPHERE

Lighting

Understand that as people age it can be much harder to see or read. Have plenty of good lighting in the party room. This is even important for some of us middle aged folks attending the party. I hate being at a party that requires any type of reading when there is not sufficient lighting. No one likes to have to strain to see, whether they are young or old. Candlelight is nice, but for an older person it can be more of an annoyance than a soother. Follow their suggestions. Ask them what they prefer.

Temperature

Consider the temperature in your home. Many elderly people don't like air conditioning. They chill much easier than younger people. Have a sweater or a shawl handy for them, or better yet give them one as a gift. Older people and young children also overheat much easier than others. Provide shade if you are having an outdoor party and it will be hot outside. Seat them under a picnic table umbrella or a tree for shade. Party tents, intended for providing shade, can be purchased at a reasonable price and used for many years. You can also rent much larger tents for a big party, but this can be costly. If it is hot, provide plenty of drinks to keep everyone cool. To keep the air moving, place some fans on a patio or a secure surface away from water. If you have outdoor ceiling fans on your porch or patio, turn them on.

Music

If the guest of honor enjoys listening to music, play their favorite songs. If the grandchildren, especially teenagers, have a problem with the choice in music, barter with them. Remind them that someday they will be old too, and to be patient for one day. Turn the music on just loud enough for everyone to hear, but not so loud that it makes talking to one another difficult.

Have you heard the song "Family Reunion" by the O'Jays? It's a great song for this party.

🎉 GAMES AND 🎉 ACTIVITIES

If the guest/guests of honor enjoys playing board games, bingo, cards, bocce ball, horseshoes or cricket, then play them. If he/she enjoys putting puzzles together, buy a new one as a gift. Have everyone join around a table in piecing together a puzzle. Make it a puzzle that is not too difficult and not too easy. Put it together on a piece of cardboard at the kitchen table or at a card table, so that when it is time to eat it can be picked up and moved out of the way. If they enjoy the water, take them on a boat ride. If you don't have a boat, you can rent one. If fishing, golfing, swimming, boating, archery or hunting is their thing, ask them if they would like to go with you. Plan a pic-

nic outing at a local park and pack their favorite foods.

Play or Make a Video

Consider playing a video from times past, if the guest of honor is not grieving over the recent loss of a loved one that would be in the videos. You may all have some good laughs. You could even make a video of the day. Interview relatives and find out how they, their parents or grandparents came to this country and why. Get your family history, memories and nationality on tape. Interview the guest of honor. Ask questions that bring up happy times from their past, such as: "What was the best thing that happened to you when you were a child?"; "Did you ever do anything wild or crazy?"; "Who was your first date?"; "How did you meet Grandma/ Grandpa?"; "What kind of games did you play when you were a kid?"; "What different jobs did you have?"; etc. They may be thrilled that you are asking these questions and love to tell their stories to you! You may have heard some of them a hundred times before, but when they are gone you will wish that you could hear them again. Who knows, they may be giving you or a relative great material to write an exciting novel.

Interview all of your relatives (aunts, uncles, parents, cousins, grandchildren) without the guest of honor's knowledge of it. If you don't see your relatives that often, conduct the interviewing during the party, and secretly in another room. Ask each family member tell something special about the guest of honor. Have them share what it is that they love about that person. Choose a grandchild to write a poem about a grandparent and recite it on video. The poem could be about the funny habits and personality traits that he/she treasures about the grandparent, or about the fun things that grandparents do with them. Make a copy of the video to give to the guest of honor and keep one for yourself. Play the video for the guest of honor during the party; they are sure to treasure it as much you and your family will.

Entertainment

Entertain the guest of honor. If it just thrills them to hear someone play the piano, guitar, flute, etc., and if you have family members or friends that play, ask them to play a song or two. Perhaps the grandchildren take dance lessons and want to show off their stuff. Let the teenagers and the little ones put together a dance routine. If it is the type of music, and the type of dance that grandma and grandpa approve of, let them strut their stuff. Have the video camera rolling!

Memory Lane

Ask grandma and grandpa to bring their photo albums to the party, if the party is not at their own home. Have them show and explain about the wonderful places they have been to, or tell about relatives that you know or don't know. Ask them to write the names of everyone in the pictures on the back of each picture, so that you will know who they are. If their writing is difficult to read, help them write down the information. You'll probably be surprised at the pictures of unique parties or places that they have been

to. Ask questions and encourage your children to ask questions. Who knows, you may be surprised to find out that grandma and grandpa were really exciting, even adventurous in their youth.

Photo Collage

Gather together photos of the guest of honor that hold a special meaning to him or her. Such photos may be their senior prom, wedding, honeymoon, births of children, family reunions, trips that they have taken, pictures of them with the grandchildren, etc. Make copies of these pictures and take them to a professional frame shop to be framed with a unique mat setting. You can even scan the photos into a computer. Following your computer manual, make a poster to hang at the party and give it to the guest of honor after the party.

Another idea would be to attach family pictures to a large painted wooden board or to make a family tree on the wooden board with the photos. Prop the board up on an easel for everyone to look at. Some office supply stores sell easels or one of your relatives may have one that you can use. My relatives put together one of these family trees for one of our family reunions and I could not believe how many family members were intrigued by it. There were relatives around it all day.

Get Those Recipes!

If your grandmother or mother is anything like mine, some of her best recipes are in her head, and not written down anywhere. When your parents or grandparents are gone, so are those recipes, unless you act quickly! Ask grandma or grandpa for all of their best recipes. Try to decipher their recipes as best as you can and make them easy to understand. To my grandmother and my mother, a pinch of salt means a lot, but to me it doesn't. You may need to get specifics from the person reciting these recipes to you. Type these recipes on a typewriter or print them up on a computer. Make photocopies of them, if you will be typing them. Make these copies into recipe books and give one to a member of each household at the party. If you like, you could even add some of your other relatives recipes that everyone always seems to enjoy at gatherings. Grandma and grandpa will be very proud that you want these recipes and glad that they will be passed down to the next generation. Many of the recipes may have already been passed down over the generations. Keep the tradition alive by making this book!

Celebrating Across the Miles

If you have grandparents that live too far away to celebrate this holiday with, you and your children can still let them know how much they mean to you by calling them, e-mailing them or sending them a Happy Grandparents Day card. They are sure to appreciate the thoughtfulness!

Halloween Party

• *October 31* •

Halloween is October 31, the eve of All Saints' Day. Halloween is a favorite day for many people young and old, and it has become one of the most important and widely celebrated festivals on today's American calendar.

How could anyone not love Halloween? Imagine a holiday that is primarily for children, it's wonderful. I can't imagine what it would have been like growing up without having been to some of the fun Halloween parties and Halloween-theme birthday parties that I attended as a child.

Plan a neighborhood gathering and take advantage of the party possibilities that this season brings. Making this a costume party would be a lot of fun. Make this a nighttime party or a slumber party and have a bonfire or a campfire. Round up your child's ghoul-friends and boo-friends for a monstrously good time! You'll have them spellbound!

🎉 PUMPKIN 🎉 INVITATION

Making a pumpkin invitation is so easy it's scary. Trace around a round cup, a pumpkin shaped cookie cutter, or a pumpkin shaped stencil on a piece of orange paper for the pumpkin shape. Cut out the shape and write on the front bottom half of the circle "You're invited!" as illustrated (fig. 26a). Draw brown lines down the front of the circle with a brown felt-tip marker (don't draw them over your words). Glue on a brown or green stem and a yellow nose, mouth and eyes. Write your invitation message on the back of the invitation somewhat like the illustration shows (fig 26b). Try to schedule your party the day before Halloween or the weekend before Halloween. Many people enjoy taking their children out trick-or-treating on Halloween. Having to worry about rushing through trick-or-treating to be to a party can put a damper on the fun of the evening. Remember when you were a child, and how much you couldn't wait to get home and dig through your bag of goodies?

(a)

(b)

Fig. 26. Pumpkin Invitation

🎉 DECORATIONS 🎉

Chances are, your home is already decorated for this holiday. Many great Halloween decorations can be found toward the end of summer and during the fall season. Below are some ideas that you may want to use, even if you already have your home decorated.

- Hang black and orange balloons and crepe paper streamers from the mailbox, front porch (away from lit pumpkins) and in the party area.

- Hang bats and ghosts from tree limbs with fishing line.

- Lay a plastic skeleton in your yard and make a gravestone for it.

- Make signs all over your lawn leading to the house that read "Danger Ahead!", "Beware!", "Haunted House" and "Turn Back NOW!" Make a sign to put next to your sidewalk that reads "Witch Crossing."

- Hang bats from fishing line across the entrance to your front porch, so that guests have to walk through them to get to your porch. Stagger them, making some high and some low to appear natural.

- Seat a stuffed scarecrow or Frankenstein on a porch chair. See game Scarecrow Making Contest for directions on how to make a scarecrow. For a Frankenstein, draw black hair on the head.

- Put a carved pumpkin on your front porch and light it for evening parties.

- Put bundles of cornstalks on each side of your front door. Tie in the center with a rope. Hang Indian corn from the rope. Indian corn can be found in the produce departments of some grocery stores during the fall season, usually after Labor Day. Place gourds and pumpkins at the base of the cornstalks.

- Put a sign on your front door that reads "Prepare yourself for a horrible scare … if you dare!"

- Hang a scary toy spider (see Craft, Black Widow Spiders) from fishing line just above the doorbell. It has a great effect! People usually pause for a moment before they ring the bell.

- Hang pictures of witches, black cats, pumpkins, bats, and ghosts in the party area and on the windows.

- Halloween tablecloths and tableware can usually be found during the Halloween season. If you can't find any, use black and orange tableware.

- For a centerpiece, place a plastic or a real Halloween pumpkin on the table. For a spooky effect, place a chunk of dry ice into a plastic pumpkin and pour water over it. It will have a very interesting smoky look to it. Dry ice can be found at welding shops and by looking under Ice in the phone directory. Watch the children very closely around the dry ice and do not allow them to touch it, since the temperature is 109° below zero. Use latex rubber gloves or tongs when handling the dry ice. Store the dry ice in the freezer or a safe place until needed. It would be best to purchase it the day of the party, if possible.

- Play scary music on your front porch as guests arrive. Later play songs like "Monster Mash" (Bobby "Boris"

Pickett & the Crypt Kickers), "The Purple People Eater" (Sheb Wooley), "Werewolves of London" (Warren Zevon), "Black Magic Woman" (Santana) or "Grim Grinning Ghosts" from the Disneyland/Walt Disney World Official Album.

The Phantom Ghost

Liven up your neighborhood this Halloween by starting a Phantom Ghost neighborhood exchange.

You will need:

2 pictures of a ghost printed from a computer or drawn

2 gift bags

2 food items (e.g., a bag of Halloween candy or a box of cookies)

2 small gifts (e.g., a Halloween decoration or Halloween candy carrying bags)

2 notes telling that the Phantom has struck

What to do:

1. Start the rumor in your neighborhood that the "Phantom" is going to be secretly visiting all of the neighbors. It is important that you do this so that word will get around about what will be happening. Otherwise, people will be getting these little surprises and be in the dark about what is going on. People may be a little leery about eating candy that has been left without knowing that it is from someone that they trust.

2. Place one picture of the phantom ghost in each gift bag,

along with one food item and one small gift. Place a note in each bag that tells the recipient that they have been struck by the "Phantom." The note should read as follows:

Goooooooooooooooood-
Eve...................ning!

The Phantom Ghost has come to town,
to leave some goodies, I see you have found
If you do not wish a curse to fall
continue this greeting, this "Phantom" call.

First, post this Phantom where it can be seen,
and leave it there till Halloween,
This will scare other Phantoms who may visit,
Be sure to participate, don't be a "fis-bidget."

Second, make two treats, two Phantoms,
and two notes like this.
Deliver them to two neighbors who may
    have been missed
Don't let them see you, be sneaky, no doubt.
And make sure they put their "Phantom
    Ghost" out.

Next, you have only one day to act, so be quick!
Leave it at doors where the Phantom has not hit.
Deliver at dark when there is no light.
Ring the doorbell, run, and stay out of sight!!

And last but not least, come join in the season.
Don't worry, be happy, you need no good reason.
Be cool, have fun and remember, don't be seen —
Share the spirit of Halloween!!!!

🎉 FOOD 🎉

There are more ideas listed here than you can possibly use, to give you many options from which to choose. Serve a warm hearty meal, if it is cold outside. See below for some ideas:

- Chili topped with shredded cheddar cheese and served with crackers

-or-

- Chicken pot pie served with baked spiced apples

-or-

- Sloppy Joes served with chips and a pickle

- Serve chip dips in small hollowed-out pumpkins

- Pumpkin shaped cookies, frosted orange or sprinkle with orange colored sugar

- Warm beverages such as hot cocoa or warm spiced apple cider are great for parties that will be held outdoors

- For an indoor party, serve Witches Brew Punch (green punch made with lime sherbet and lemon lime soda), or if you prefer just use green colored Kool Aid. For an eerie looking effect, make ice shaped hands to place in the punch bowl by pouring water in 2 food handler's plastic gloves (not latex gloves with talcum powder); tie tightly closed with a rubber band to hold water in. Place the water filled gloves in a bowl, with the tied ends pointed up, and freeze. When frozen solid, carefully remove the plastic gloves and refreeze the ice hand shapes until the party. During the party, set the frozen "hands" in the punch bowl. This punch will really have your guests talking!

Baked Pumpkin Seeds

You will need:

2 cups of pumpkin seeds from a
    medium sized pumpkin

3 Tbsp. melted butter

1 tsp. Worcestershire sauce,
    optional

1 tsp. salt

What to do:

1. After you have carved your Halloween pumpkin, and scooped the seeds out of the pumpkin, place them in a colander, rinse the orange pulp off of them, and drain.

2. Dry the seeds on a dishcloth and cover with another. Leave on the counter to dry overnight.

3. When the seeds have dried, toss them in a medium bowl with the Worcestershire sauce, melted butter and salt. Stir until coated.

4. Spread out on a cookie sheet and bake at 350° for 15–20 minutes or until golden brown and crisp. Stir once or twice to prevent scorching.

5. Allow to cool. Store tightly covered for up to two weeks. Makes 2 cups.

Jack-o-Lantern I-Screams

Make these unique ice cream balls at least a day or more before the party.

You will need:

Paper cupcake liners
Orange sherbet
Chocolate chips
Chocolate kisses
Black or chocolate licorice twist

What to do:

1. Flatten out paper cupcake liners and set them on top of a cookie sheet.

2. Scoop rounded balls of orange sherbet and set one on top of each flattened paper cupcake liner. If you have a small freezer, you may need to set the ice cream in muffin tin cups or in a small pan.

3. Use two chocolate chips for the eyes, one chocolate kiss pushed in for the nose, and a cut piece of licorice for the mouth.

4. Place in the freezer uncovered. After the ice cream has set, you may want to cover it with a plastic bag, if it will be a long time before it will be served.

Variation: The ice cream can also be placed in a scooped out orange. Cut off the top ¼ of the orange and remove the orange pulp. Cut out a pumpkin-type face from the orange rind, or draw one on the rind with a pen. Fill the orange with the orange sherbet or chocolate ice cream and if desired, replace the top of the orange. Store covered in the freezer until needed.

Kitty I-Screams

Make these adorable ice cream balls at least a day or more before the party.

You will need:

Paper cupcake liners

Chocolate, vanilla or orange ice cream

Chocolate kisses

Small green, round candies (such as M&M's)

Small round red or pink candy

Black or red string licorice

What to do:

1. Flatten out paper cupcake liners and set them on top of a cookie sheet.

2. Scoop rounded balls of the chosen ice cream and set the ice cream on top of the paper liners. If you have a small freezer, you may need to set the ice cream in a muffin tin or on a smaller pan.

3. Use two chocolate kisses for the kitty ears, green candy for the eyes, red or pink candy for the nose, and string licorice for the mouth and whiskers.

Witches' Hats

When your guests ask you how you made these eye-catching cookies, they will be shocked at how incredibly simple they are to make!

You will need:

Keeblers fudge striped cookies or other fudge striped cookies
Hersheys chocolate kisses
A tube of orange decorators icing

What to do:

1. Turn the cookie upside down, so that the chocolate side faces up.

2. Pipe orange frosting around the center hole of each cookie.

3. Place an unwrapped kiss on the icing.

4. Pipe a thin band of frosting around the base of the kiss and pipe a little bow on the kiss. See illustration (fig. 27).

Fig. 27. Witches' Hats

Ghost Cookies

You will need:

1 package of Nutter Butter cookies (shaped like a peanut)
1 lb. white chocolate
1 tube of chocolate decorator icing or black gel icing
Waxed paper

What to do:

1. In a large microwave-safe bowl, heat the white chocolate until melted (about 2 minutes).

2. Dip cookies in melted chocolate, and lay them in a single layer on waxed paper.

3. Pipe ghost eyes and a mouth onto each cookie with icing. Let the cookies set until the chocolate hardens.

Lollipop Ghosts

These make great party favors and can also be used as a party craft project with the children. Since these are so simple and inexpensive to make, they are great for school Halloween parties.

You will need:

Round ball-type lollipops
White facial tissue paper or white
material
Black or orange yarn
Black felt tip marker or craft wiggle
eyes
Glue, optional

What to do:

1. Cover the lollipop with a tissue
or a square of material.

2. Tie a piece of yarn at the top of
the stick and just under the ball
of candy.

3. Draw eyes onto the "ghost
head" with marker or glue on
wiggle eyes.

Spooky Halloween Hands

If you need to make a lot of these,
allow your children to help you out.
They will enjoy helping you make them
and things will go a lot faster.

You will need:

Candy corn, green jelly beans, or
black jelly beans
Popcorn
Clear disposable gloves (food handler gloves work best; don't use
latex gloves with talcum powder
in them)
Plastic spider rings, optional
Black or orange ribbon or yarn

What to do:

1. Stuff 1 candy corn or 1 jellybean
(all of one color) into each
finger of the glove for the
fingernails.

2. Fill the rest of the glove with
popcorn, and tie the open end
closed with the ribbon or yarn.

3. Slip a spider ring on the ring
finger, if desired.

Halloween Caramel Apple Faces

If you have a lot of guests, you
may need to double, triple, or even
quadruple this recipe.

One 14-oz. pkg. (49) caramel candies
2 Tbsp. water
4 or 5 medium apples
4 or 5 wooden sticks
M & M's candies
Candy corn
Skittles candies
Yellow food coloring or other desired color

What to do:

1. Insert a wooden stick into the
stem end of each apple.

2. In top of double boiler or
saucepan, combine caramels
and water. Cook over low heat
until melted, stirring occasion-
ally. Remove from heat.

3. Dip apples into caramel mixture, turning to coat. Scrape off
excess caramel mixture when
removing apple from pan. Place
on greased waxed paper.

4. When cooled, pour food coloring on top of caramel apple for
the hair and close to the stick.

5. Push 2 M & M's on the middle
of the apple for the eyes. Push
on a piece of candy corn for the

nose. Push the 5 or 6 Skittles on for the mouth.

Yield, 4–5 apples.

Pumpkin Cake

You will need:

3 boxes of cake mix, plus ingredients as box directs

2 Bundt cake pans (or, use one twice)

2 16-oz. cans of vanilla frosting

Orange food coloring

Yellow fruit roll snacks

Chocolate frosting or a tube of black gel frosting, optional

Plastic wrap

1 round chocolate Ho-Ho or other similar round chocolate snack cake

Green mint candy leaves, optional

What to do:

1. Mix cake mixes according to directions. Pour ½ of the cake batter into a greased and floured Bundt pan, or if you have two pans of the same size, pour half of the cake batter into one pan and the other half into another. Bake and cool both cakes according to package directions.

2. Color the vanilla frosting orange with the food coloring.

3. Trim the bottoms (not the rounded sides) of the Bundt cakes making them flat, so that they will fit together smoothly.

4. Place one cake on a serving platter flat side up. Spread the flat side with orange frosting.

5. Place the other cake flat side down over the first cake, lining up any ridges, so that they match. This will now appear round, as a pumpkin.

6. Stuff the center hole with plastic wrap to just below the top. This is to help keep the chocolate snack cake in place as the pumpkin stem.

7. Spread the remaining orange frosting on the entire cake.

8. Cut 3 large triangles from the yellow fruit roll snack for the eyes and nose, and cut a pumpkin-type mouth. Get creative, make it spooky, if you like. For easier cutting, use a clean straight edge razor. Slightly press the cut shapes onto the icing to hold in place.

9. Place the round chocolate snack cake on top of the cake, over the hole, creating a stem.

10. If desired, frost black or chocolate vertical lines from the top of the cake to the bottom, to appear as pumpkin stripes.

11. Place the mint candy leaves on the top of the pumpkin around the "stem."

Variation: Use an ice cream cone for the stem and frost it brown or green. Sometimes colored ice cream cones can be found. If you can find a green cone, use that.

Spider Cake

You will need:

1 box of cake mix, plus ingredients
  as box directs
Chocolate frosting
Blue food coloring, optional
Black or chocolate licorice strips
Large black gumdrops
Red fruit roll snack
Yellow fruit roll snack
Green gumballs, optional

What to do:

1. Preheat oven to 350°. Prepare
   batter according to package directions and pour into a
   greased and floured 2 quart
   ovenproof bowl. Bake for
   55–65 minutes, or until cake
   tester inserted in center comes
   out clean. Cool 15 minutes on
   cooling rack; invert. Cool 3–4
   hours before decorating.

2. Place the cake on a foil-covered
   board, rounded side up. Frost
   the entire cake with chocolate
   frosting. If you would like a
   dark brown spider cake, mix
   the chocolate icing with some
   blue food coloring before frosting the cake.

3. Cut out a crescent shape from
   the red fruit roll snack for the
   mouth. Cut out triangles from
   the yellow fruit roll snack for
   the fangs, and place them below
   the mouth. Slightly press the
   cut shapes onto the icing to
   hold them in place.

4. Cut out two circles from the
   yellow fruit roll snack for the

eyes, or use two green gumballs
for eyes.

5. Cut 8-inch pieces from the
   licorice for the legs. Stick one
   end of each leg into the body.
   Cut a slit into each gumdrop,
   and stick the other end of each
   leg into one. The gumdrops re-
   sembling the feet.

Creepy Cupcakes

You will need:

1 package of chocolate cake mix,
  plus ingredients as box directs
Paper cupcake liners, 2 per cupcake
1 package of black or chocolate
  string licorice
1 16 oz. container of chocolate frosting
Blue food coloring, optional
1 large bag of M & M's candies

What to do:

1. Bake and cool cupcakes in 1
   paper liner each as directed.

2. Remove the paper cupcake liners from all of the cupcakes.

3. If you would like to make the
   chocolate frosting a dark
   brown, add blue food coloring
   to it and mix well. This would
   only be necessary if you are
   using the black string licorice.

4. Place each cupcake on top of a
   new paper cupcake liner, with
   the large end down.

5. Push 8 cut pieces of licorice
   into the sides of each cupcake
   to resemble spider legs. Place 4
   on one side and 4 on the other
   side. See illustration (fig. 28).

6. Make eyes with 2 green or yellow M & M's.

Fig. 28. Creepy Cupcakes

🎉 ARRIVAL 🎉 OF GUESTS

Elevator Antics

If you live in an apartment complex with an elevator, have two people stand in the elevator. Have one person dressed as an angel and the other dressed as the devil. As each guest enters the elevator, have the devil ask real eerily, "Going down?" and have the angel ask real sweetly, "Going up?" This should cause much laughter — or send your guests running to the stairs! You should get permission from the apartment complex manager before playing this prank. Some of your fellow tenants may not have as good of a sense of humor as you have.

Halloween Talk

If this party is not a costume party, seat everyone in a circle as they arrive, and ask each child to tell what they plan on wearing for Halloween. Ask everyone what their favorite Halloween candy is and what they like best about Halloween.

🎉 CRAFTS 🎉

Decorate Your Own Monster Cookie

You will need:

Large, round home baked cookies or packaged cookies

1 or 2 16-oz. cans of white frosting

Green or yellow food coloring, optional

Plastic zippered sandwich bags, 1 per child, optional

Scissors, optional

Various assorted candies: candy corn, chocolate sprinkles, gumdrops, string licorice, jellybeans, fruit roll snacks, marshmallows, M & M's, etc.

What to do:

1. Before the party, empty one can of frosting into a bowl and color it yellow. Empty the other can into another bowl and color it green. If desired, put a little frosting into individual sandwich bags to make decorating bags for the frosting, or keep the two colors in separate bowls for the children to spread the frosting on their cupcakes. Put the candies into individual bowls.

2. During the party, set all of the items on the table or counter. Snip off a small corner of each bag to make a piping bag. If using the bowls of frosting, place a few butter knives into each bowl.

3. Let the children decorate their cookies to look like scary monsters, creatures or spiders. Let them use the frosting for the background to the faces, or use it like glue to stick the candy pieces onto the faces. Use candy corn for hair, ears or fangs; chocolate sprinkles for hair or a beard; gumdrops for bulging eyes; string licorice for hair, legs, whiskers or mouths; jellybeans for nose or eyes; fruit rolls for hair, eyes, mouths or ears; marshmallows for teeth; M & M's for eyes, nose or mouth. The children may eat their creations, or wrap them in cellophane to take home after the party.

Pumpkin Decorating Contest

You will need:

Small pumpkins or gourds, 1 per child

Permanent marker

Acrylic paints

Disposable bowls

Paintbrushes, 1 per child, if possible

Newspaper

What to do:

1. Label the bottom of each child's pumpkin with their name, using permanent marker and allow it to dry.

2. Spread the newspaper out on a table or on the ground. Place paintbrushes and individual bowls of different colored paints on top of the newspaper.

Pass out the pumpkins and tell the children to paint anything they like on the pumpkin.

Note: Forewarn parents on the invitation that you will be painting, if you decide to do this craft, so that they may send their children in playclothes.

Black Widow Spider Puppets

For this craft, you will need one adult or teen helper for about every 3 or 4 children, depending on the age group of your guests.

You will need:

4 black pipe cleaners, per guest

1 black 2-inch pompom, per guest

2-foot piece of fishing line, one per guest

Popsicle sticks or craft sticks, 1 per guest

Stapler

¼-inch wiggle eyes, 2 per guest

Glue

Red shiny metallic origami paper or red construction paper

Scissors

What to do:

1. Have each child take four pipe cleaners and twist them on the underside of the pompom.

2. Pull the pipe cleaners apart to appear as spider legs. Bend the tips of each leg out at about 1 inch from the end.

3. Tie one end of the fishing line onto the top half of the spider, by tying it to the legs.

4. Tie the other end of the fishing line to the popsicle stick or craft stick. Staple the fishing line to the stick to secure it.

5. Glue the wiggle eyes in place.

6. Cut an hourglass shape from the origami paper or construction paper. Glue it onto the top of the pompom. You now have a black widow spider ready to scare an unsuspecting victim!

Shadow Puppets

See Chinese New Year. Make ghosts, witches, cats, etc. After the puppets are made, it would be fun to use them at an evening party or around a campfire. Just watch and make sure that the children keep the puppets away from the fire.

Leaf Rubbings

See May Day Festival/Spring Party.

GAMES AND ACTIVITIES

Halloween Costume Contest

After everyone has arrived, have a costume contest. Ask everyone to model their costume in front of the group. Award a prize for every costume. Award a piece of candy for the scariest, cutest, funniest, most unique, most effort, most elaborate, prettiest, etc.

Haunted House

If you have a garage or basement, turn it into a haunted house. Recruit some teenagers that you know to help run the haunted house. Let them come up with some ideas (not too scary) and dress up in costumes. Change the light bulbs in the "haunted house" to black light bulbs. Hang black plastic tarps or dye old sheets black to hang in a maze-like fashion. Have the children walk through the maze, and let each section of the maze have a different theme. Ask someone to dress in a witch's costume, and stand, stirring a black, smoking witch's cauldron (to create a smoking effect, see Decorations). Give the witch a made-up witch's potion to recite as the children walk past her. She could eerily say something like, "Double bubble boil of trouble. Ehh ehh ehh!" Another child could wrap torn strips of an old sheet around himself and pretend to be a mummy by walking with outstretched arms and possibly dragging one leg behind him. Have the mummy moan and groan. Someone could lie in a very large cardboard box (e.g., a refrigerator box) and pretend that it is a coffin. Have him paint his face and hands white to look like a corpse and wear long black fake nails. Paint a ping-pong ball to look like an eyeball or purchase one of these fake eyeballs and have him hold it up to his face. As each child walks up to the coffin, have the "dead person" sit up and pretend that he lost his eyeball by dropping it on the ground. Have him ask each child if he/she would help find his eyeball for him. Some will be too scared to pick it up, and others will be like I was as a child when this happened to me at a haunted house. I reached down, picked it up, handed it to the monster and laughed, much to my parent's surprise. They're still joking about it, and that was many, many years ago! Whatever you choose to do, have fun with it!

Haunted Hayride

This is a hayride that may be more suitable for older children. It may be too scary for some young children. Take younger children on a hayride without the monsters. Although my neighborhood hosts a monster hayride for the children every year, and all of the children think that it is fun, you may have a guest or two who won't feel that way. Recruit your teen volunteers from the haunted house to stand in an area as your sub and wait for you to bring the children in a hay filled trailer. If you don't have a trailer, see if a friend or relative has one that they can loan to you for the day. Place an adult in the trailer with the children as someone slowly drives the children to the site where the teenagers are waiting. Once you get there, give them a brief moment to do their thing, and remind them not to make it too scary. Happy Haunting!

Take a Trip

Take a trip to a pumpkin patch. Some pumpkin farms have hayrides to take you out to the field. Once you reach the field, the children all get to pick their own pumpkin to take home. It is so fun to pick out your own pumpkin in a real pumpkin patch. Some pumpkin farms have cider mills or cider presses and you can watch them make fresh cider. You could pack a lunch and have a picnic there. Eat on a blanket or out on the tailgate. You might even consider taking everyone back to your home afterwards for a meal or a snack served with some hot cocoa. Play some games and play the Pumpkin Decorating Contest.

Spooky Story Contest

If the children won't be dressing in costumes, you may want to do this activity around a campfire. If they will be dressed in costumes, you should only do this around a pretend campfire, for safety reasons. Seat all of the children in a circle around the real or pretend campfire. Starting with an adult or the birthday child, move clockwise around the circle and have each person tell a spooky or funny Halloween story.

Wrap Up the Mummy Contest

You will need:

2 full rolls of toilet paper

What to do:

1. Divide the children into 2 equal teams and hand each team a roll of toilet paper.

2. The teams must choose one child from their group to be the "mummy." The 2 chosen children should be of equal size. It wouldn't be fair if one team had a tiny 3-year-old child to dress and the other had a tall 12 year old to dress. Usually one child will gladly volunteer.

3. At the signal to go, all of the team members join in wrap-

ping the roll of toilet paper around the "mummy." The first team to completely wrap up the mummy wins.

Note: You can recycle the toilet paper, by using it in the Scarecrow-Making contest.

Scarecrow Making Contest

You will need:

2 old flannel or plaid shirts

2 old pair of jeans

2 pair of gloves, optional

2 pair of old socks, optional

Rubber bands, optional

2 paper or cloth bags with a face drawn on them

2 old straw hats, optional

Stuffing: Lots of newspaper (if activity is indoors), hay or straw (if activity is outdoors)

Clothespins

What to do:

1. Divide the children into two equal teams. Give each team equal amounts of items.

2. On the signal to go, they are to stuff their team's scarecrow with chosen stuffing. They must button the shirt, and attach it to the pants with the clothespins. After they stuff the head, have them stick it into the neck of the shirt, and put the straw hat on it. They arc to use the rubber bands to attach the socks to the pants and the gloves to the shirt. The first team to finish wins!

Leaf Pile Treasure Hunt

Before the party, rake up a big pile of leaves, and remove any sticks or pinecones. Hide several inexpensive toys in the pile of leaves. During the party, let the children search all at once through the pile of leaves on a signal to go.

Dangling Donuts

You will need:

A long rope

Clean string or yarn

Donuts, 1 per child

What to do:

1. Before the party, suspend the rope between two trees or across a room. Since this is a messy game, you may prefer to play it outdoors. Tie on one piece of string for every child, about a foot or two long, from the suspended rope. Keep the strings about two feet apart. Make sure that you hang some lower than others for shorter guests. Tie a donut onto the end of each string.

2. During the party, line all of the children up in front of a donut. At the signal to go, they must all try to eat their donut, with their hands behind their backs the entire time. The first child to finish his donut wins.

Bobbing for Apples

Now a Halloween party just would not be complete without this game. As a parent, I cringe at the thought of germs. But from a child's point of view the thought is, "Who cares! I'm having fun Ma!" Watching my kids play this game with all of their friends every Halloween and having a great time, brings back good memories from my own childhood. I guess I'll have to forget my germ phobia for this game, and just sit back and enjoy the show!

You will need:

A large metal or plastic tub filled with water (you can line it with a clean plastic garbage bag that has been taped on, if necessary)

1 apple per child

What to do:

1. Place the tub on the ground outdoors (e.g., garage or driveway), if possible, since it will make a mess. Place the apples in the tub of water.

2. Line the children up single file. Each child takes a turn at kneeling down in front of the tub of water and tries to bite into an apple, to remove it from the tub, while keeping their hands behind their back. If desired, tie their hands with a bandanna. They get to keep and eat their apple as a prize.

Caution: Never leave small children unattended around the tub of water. It would be a good idea to have two strong men take the tub away from the party area after the game, and dump out the water. This is especially important if there will be toddlers at the party. All it takes is a second for them to fall into the water.

Bat Cave

You will need:

Card table
Large blanket
Several clothespins
Plastic toy bats
Clear fishing line
Treats: Halloween pencils, candy, spider rings, fake witch nails, Dracula teeth, etc.
Flashlight

What to do:

1. Before the party, cover the card table with the blanket, leaving one end open to resemble a cave opening. Secure the blanket with clothespins.

2. Hang some plastic bats from the entrance to the "cave" with fishing line.

3. Place some candy or novelty items in the cave.

4. During the party, send the children into the cave with a flashlight to search for *one* goody. When they come out, make sure that one is all they have taken or you may not have enough for the rest of the children. You may want to use the cave as a place where the children go to collect a prize after a game, or use it after the children are out of the game Hot Apple.

Hide and Ghost Seek

Make little ghosts out of white facial tissues by stuffing the center with a rolled ball of tissue and tie a piece of string around the neck. Draw on the eyes nose and mouth with a black felt tip marker. Loosely hang the ghosts around the house or yard with string or tape, so that they can be easily pulled down, or just hide them without hanging them. At a signal to go, send the children to seek the ghosts. The child to find the most ghosts wins a prize.

Hot Apple

This game is played just like Hot Potato. See St. Patrick's Party for directions to this game. An appropriate prize for this game would be a candy apple or a small sack of apples for the winner. Give an apple-flavored sucker to each child as they are out, or send them to the bat cave.

Candy Corn Guess

See Easter Party Games, Jellybean Guess.

Nut Gathering Contest

See Thanksgiving Party. This is a game that may need to be played at a daytime party, so that it can be played outdoors. You could play it indoors, if you purchase a bag of unshelled nuts to hide indoors.

Goody Holder Ideas

During the Halloween season, it should be easy to find Halloween goody bags or even inexpensive plastic pumpkins to put your party favors in. You may even be able to find small black witches cauldrons or kettles. These are also great for the St. Patrick's Party, but can't be found at that time of the year. So, if you are planning on having a St. Patrick's Party, be sure to get your kettles near the Halloween season. If you would like to keep your goody bag cost low, decorate a plain brown paper lunch bag with acrylic paint or construction paper. Put pumpkins, witches, bats or ghosts on them.

FAVOR AND PRIZE IDEAS

Plastic spider rings, fake witch nails, Dracula teeth, Halloween theme items (erasers, pencils, lapel pins, stickers, magnets, etc.), caramel apples, candy apples, caramel popcorn balls, candy corn, bubble gum eyeballs, sacks of apples, apple flavor candy, Lollipop Ghosts (see Food), Monster Cookies (see Crafts), Decorated Pumpkins (see Crafts), Black Widow Spider Puppets (see Crafts), Shadow Puppets (see Crafts) or Leaf Rubbings (see Crafts).

Thanksgiving Party

• *4th Thursday in November* •

Thanksgiving is a time when family and friends gather together to feast and give thanks for what they have received in the previous year. Prayers are expressed for a good year, good health, and prosperity.

The first American Thanksgiving was celebrated in 1621, one year after the Pilgrims landed at Plymouth Rock. This day was very meaningful to the Pilgrims, because they had such a difficult year before that. Many of the new settlers had died and food was scarce. So the Pilgrims certainly had much to be thankful for when they reaped a bountiful fall harvest.

It wasn't until November 26, 1789, 168 years after the first American Thanksgiving, that this holiday was proclaimed as a day of thanksgiving and prayer. In 1863, Thanksgiving was made an official annual holiday by President Abraham Lincoln.

If you are planning a Thanksgiving themed party, event, or family gathering and want to make it special, then check out the following pages of this chapter. In it you'll find many great ideas that can be used from year to year. Your child might think that this is a great theme for a school or church party, especially if your child likes to do crafts. This chapter certainly has an abundance of craft ideas to choose from. If Thanksgiving dinner is at your home this year, and young children will be coming, have a teenager or adult keep the children busy with some of the ideas listed in this chapter. That will help you out tremendously while trying to prepare dinner. It may also give older relatives a chance to talk with one another or even join in and play with the children. Celebrate each Thanksgiving holiday in a unique way by making a traditional Colonial American or Thanksgiving-themed craft and playing fun games. Whether celebrating with friends or having relatives over for a traditional feast, create some lasting memories with the ideas in this chapter; you'll be "thankful" you did.

🎉 TURKEY 🎉 INVITATION

Trace the shape of your child's hand, with his fingers spread out, on a piece of light brown paper (a brown paper grocery bags works well). Cut out the hand shape. Draw an eye on the thumb of the invitation. Cut out a tiny orange paper triangle and glue it onto the thumb end as a beak. Cut out a red paper throat wattle and glue it under the chin of the turkey. See illustration (fig. 29). If desired, cut out different colored fingers to glue onto the fingers of the turkey, to resemble the colored

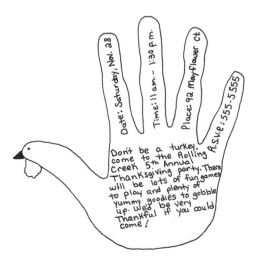

Fig. 29. Turkey Invitation

feathers of a turkey. Write the date, time, place and RSVP on the fingers. Write the message on the palm of the hand, something like the sample illustration (fig. 29).

🎉 DECORATIONS 🎉

During the Thanksgiving season, many holiday-related decorations can be found in stores. Below are some ideas for you to use at a Thanksgiving party in addition to what may be found in the stores.

- Use yellow, orange, red and brown balloons and crepe paper streamers to decorate the mailbox, front porch and party area.

- Lawn signs can be made or purchased that have a Thanksgiving theme. Make one that reads "Turkey Crossing" and place it next to your driveway or sidewalk.

- Hang Indian corn from the light fixtures on your front porch. Place one on each side of the front door.

- Put bundles of cornstalks on each side of your front door. Tie in the center with a rope and hang Indian corn from the rope. Indian corn can be found in the produce department of some grocery stores during the fall season. Place gourds at the base of each cornstalk.

- Put a picture of a turkey on the front door. Make the turkey from construction paper or print one from a computer. Write "Happy Thanksgiving" under the picture of the turkey.

Laminate the picture so that you can reuse it for many years.

- Trace your child's hand to make turkey shapes. Let him decorate them with crayons or markers, and hang them all over the house. Make pictures of pilgrim hats (complete with the buckled hat strap), Pilgrims, boats that look like the *Mayflower*, American Indians or Indian corn. Hang the pictures in the party area.
- Thanksgiving tablecloths and tableware can be found in many stores during the fall season. You can also use an orange tablecloth with brown, red or yellow tableware.
- Purchase a turkey centerpiece and put it on the center of the table, or put a cornucopia basket filled with gourds in the center of the table.
- For placecards at the party table, have your child write a short note or poem to each guest. On it he can write why he is thankful for that friend or relative. Another placecard idea would be to use turkey shaped cookies. Frost each guest's name on his cookie.

Cornucopia or Horn of Plenty

Have you ever wondered why the horned shaped baskets filled with fruits and vegetables are a symbol of Thanksgiving? Well, since ancient times this has been a symbol of harvest and good crops. The shape itself comes from ancient Greek folklore and recalls the practice of decorating a goat's horns with flowers, fruits, and corn. If the goat was dressed for the harvest festival, it was believed that he would never want for anything. Hollow goats horns were also filled with fruit and flowers and were presented to the nymph Amalthaea. To this day, the horn shape is a symbol of abundance and an overflowing supply.

FOOD

If this will be a school, church, or birthday party, you may want to use the menu below. If this will be a traditional family gathering, then I am sure that you and your family will have plenty of your own ideas in mind for a meal. Ask each relative to bring a covered dish to share and to help lighten your workload.

- Turkey sandwiches
- Potato salad
- Gelatin mold, applesauce or sliced apples
- Popcorn
- One or two types of pies: Pumpkin, Sweet Potato, Apple, Pecan, etc.

Turkey Cupcakes

You will need:

Baked cupcakes
1 16-oz. can of white frosting
Orange food coloring
Round vanilla sandwich cookies or round crackers
Chocolate kisses
Candy corn
Caramel squares

What to do:

1. Bake and cool the cupcakes according to directions.

2. Reserve a small amount of the white frosting (about ¼ cup). Color the remaining frosting orange. Frost the tops of the cupcakes with the orange frosting.

3. Spread some white frosting on a cookie or a cracker.

4. Place a chocolate kiss near the bottom of the cracker.

5. Add the candy corn to the frosting around the kiss to create the turkey "feathers." Arrange the candy corn pointed side in and wide side out. Place one candy corn on the kiss for the head, using frosting to attach. Place the pointed side facing out (near the pointed end of the chocolate kiss). Make one of these turkeys for each cupcake. Allow the frosting to dry.

6. Attach a caramel to the back of the cookie or cracker with

Fig. 30. Turkey Cupcakes

frosting to create a little stand. Let it dry.

7. Place one turkey on top of each frosted cupcake. See illustration (fig. 30).

☗ CRAFTS ☗

Pilgrim Hat Candy Holders

This is a craft that you may want to make before the party for your guests. These little hats make great candy or nut holders. Make one for each guest or place a few filled cups on tables for guests to nibble out of.

You will need:

1 black disposable cup (usually found near the "Over the Hill" party supplies)

Black construction paper or a black disposable plate, for the hat rim

Glue

Scissors

Yellow construction paper

What to do:

1. Cut the bottom of the cup out.

2. If using black construction paper for the hat rim, cut it a little larger than the lip of the cup, in a circle. Use a bowl for a template and trace around it to make the circle.

3. Glue the lip of the cup to the construction paper or to the black plate.

4. If desired, cut a black strip of paper to go around the lower end of the hat, to look like a hat strap.

5. Cut a square out of the yellow construction paper, and cut a smaller square out of its center, creating the strap buckle. Glue the buckle to the strap. Allow all pieces to dry. You now have a pilgrim hat ready to be filled with goodies!

Turkey Placemats

18 × 24-inch sheets of white paper or light brown construction paper, 1 per child

Crayons

A cardboard turkey shape for tracing, optional

What to do:

As the children arrive, keep them busy by making placemats. Have them trace a turkey shape or draw their own. If they want to, they can write on the turkey what they are thankful for, or they may just color in the turkey shape. Write the children's names on the turkeys and tape their turkey in the spot that they will be sitting in.

Indian Corn Wreaths

You will need:

Dried ears of corn (check with a produce market or the produce department of a grocery store)

Picture wire cut to 3 feet, 1 per child

A hand saw

A drill

A pair of pliers

What to do:

1. Before the party, saw the dried corn into 2-inch pieces. Drill holes through the center of the corn (through the woody-type part).

2. During the party, let the children string the wire through the holes of the corn. Watch them closely. If they are very young, an adult will need to help each child, so that they don't poke their eyes or others' eyes with the wire.

3. Twist the two wire ends together with pliers for the children, making sure that there aren't any sharp points sticking out. They now have a corn wreath for decorating their front door or for placing out in the yard for the animals.

Pinecone Birdfeeders

You will need:

Pinecones (if you can find large ones, that would be great), 1 per child

String cut to 15 inches long, 1 per child

Newspaper

Popsicle sticks found at a craft store

Paper plates, 1 per child

Inexpensive peanut butter or solid vegetable shortening (hardened fat drippings will work also)

Bags to take the feeders home in, 1 per child

1 large paper grocery bag

Birdseed (preferably the type with sunflower seeds in the mix)

What to do:

1. Cover a table or floor with the newspaper to protect the work area from any sticky messes or spills.

2. Give each child a pinecone and a piece of string.

3. Pass out a paper plate to each child, with a popsicle stick and a scoop of peanut butter or vegetable shortening on it. Make the scoop about ⅓–½ cup, depending on the size of the pinecones. Instruct the children not to eat the peanut butter or vegetable shortening. They will try, trust me.

4. Tell the children to scoop the peanut butter or shortening with the popsicle stick and put it on the pinecone. Make sure that they put plenty of it on the pinecone.

5. Put some birdseed in the large paper grocery bag. As the children finish putting the peanut butter or shortening on the pinecone, take their pinecone and shake it in the bag of bird seed. The seeds will stick to the pinecone. Shake off any loose seeds.

6. Tightly tie the string into a knot at the top of the pinecone and place the pinecone in a bag labeled with the child's name. Instruct the children to hang the bird feeders on a tree, bush or fence when they get home. Maybe near a window so that they can watch the birds come to "their" feeders.

Caution: Some children may be allergic to peanut butter, so be sure to let the parents know what you will be doing before you have any of the children begin.

Corn Husk Dolls

This Native American craft makes a great Thanksgiving decoration. The Colonists learned to make these dolls from the American Indians. Corn husk dolls were made by Iroquois Indians after their harvest festivals. The dolls were made by the adults for the children. The Iroquois did not put faces on their dolls, because they believe that only the creator can make a face.

In Colonial America, people lived mostly on farms. There were very few stores and they sold only necessities like food, tools and clothing. So toys had to be made at home from materials that were available such as the corn husks. These dolls may not have been as fancy as today's dolls, but they were much loved and played with.

You will need:

Dry corn husks or tamale wrappers (found in Mexican markets)
String
Scissors
Cotton balls
Pipe cleaners

What to do:

1. Soak the corn husks in a large pot or bucket of warm water until they become pliable (about 1 hour).

2. Take 6 large husks, squeeze out the water, and drain them on a

towel. Lay them on top of one another, with the large ends at the top. Tie them together tightly about 1 inch from the top. Cut the edges, shaping the top into a rounded head. See illustration (fig. 31a).

3. Holding the head, turn upside down and pull husks, one at a time, over the head. Tie a piece of string around the husks, at the top, to form the neck. See illustration (fig. 31b).

4. Take one husk, place a piece of pipe cleaner on it, and roll it inside of the husk to create the arms. Tie a piece of string about ½ inch from each end, and tie another at the center. Trim ends of string.

5. Place a cotton ball around the center of the arm piece. Separate the husks of the body and place the arm piece up under the neck. See illustration (fig. 31c). Hold the arms in place by tying a piece of string in an "X" across the chest and back of the doll. See illustration (fig. 31d).

6. Take two pieces of husks, about 1 inch wide, and fold one over the left shoulder and one over the right shoulder of the doll. Cross them like an "X" at the front and back waist of the doll and tie at the waist. See illustration (fig. 31e).

7. Take 5 or 6 husks and place them with the large ends above the dolls head and the narrow ends just below the waist. Overlap them and arrange them as evenly as you can all around

the doll waist. Tie them at the waist, still above the doll head, to secure. See illustration (fig. 31f).

8. Fold the husks down to form a skirt. See illustration (fig. 31g). Trim the arms and skirt edges. To make a boy doll, cut a slit up the center of the skirt, and tie at the knees and the ankles to create legs. Allow the dolls to dry naturally. You now have a corn husk doll ready for playing or decorating!

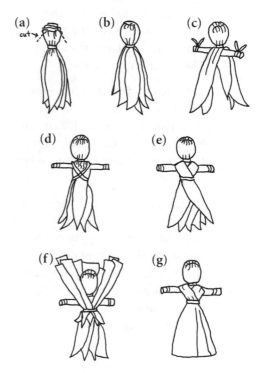

Fig. 31. Corn Husk Dolls

Pinecone Turkeys

You will need:

Small pinecones, 1 per child
Turkey head shapes cut from thin

cardboard (cut in an oval shape and then cut one end pointed)

Craft wiggle eyes (found at craft stores)

Small colorful dyed duck quill feathers (found at craft stores)

Red and yellow construction paper

Glue

What to do:

1. Glue the wiggle eyes near the rounded part of the head. Cut and glue a red wattle to the lower half (the pointed end) of the head. Cut out a yellow beak and glue it onto the head. Lay the pinecone on its side and glue the head onto the large end of the pinecone.

2. Cut out a pair of webbed feet from the yellow paper and glue them onto the lower half of the cone.

3. Put some glue onto the end of several different colored feathers and stick the feathers into the back of the pinecone (or the pointed end). Stick the feathers straight out to resemble the feathers of a turkey.

Apple Turkeys

You will need:

Apples, 1 per child

Toothpicks, several per child

Colorful gummy worms, several per child

2 white paper turkey head shapes (one for the left side and one for the right side), 1 set per child

Crayons

What to do:

1. Have the children draw a face on the turkey head and the glue the two head pieces together onto a toothpick. Lay apple on its side and push the toothpick into the bottom end of the apple. See illustration (fig. 32).

2. Push one gummy worm onto each toothpick. Leave half of the toothpick exposed. Make about 7–10 of these per turkey. Push the other end of the toothpick into the apple, at the opposite side of the head, to create the tail feathers of the turkey. See illustration (fig. 32). You now have a turkey that looks good enough to gobble up!

Fig. 32. Apple Turkeys

Make Your Own Turkey Cookie

You will need:

Baked gingerbread cookies that have been cut with a hand shaped cookie cutter, 1 per child

White icing

Red food coloring, optional

Plastic zippered sandwich bags, 1 per child

Candy corn

M & M's candies

What to do:

1. Before the party, put the white icing in individual sandwich bags and seal them shut. If you like, color a small amount of icing red to have one bag of red icing for decorating the turkey wattles.

2. During the party, set all of the supplies out on a table or countertop. Snip off a small corner of each bag of frosting to create decorator bags.

3. Give each child a cookie to decorate. Let them use the icing like glue to hold the candies onto the hand shaped cookie. Use the M & M's candies to decorate the fingers of the hands like colorful feathers. Place one candy corn on the thumb as the turkey's beak. Use a small dot of frosting for an eye. If using the red frosting, decorate a red turkey wattle under the beak.

4. If the children like, they can frost their names on the turkey body. Set these aside and allow to them dry before wrapping them up to take home, or let the children eat them.

Note: Hand shaped cookie cutters can be found in craft and kitchen supply stores. If you can't find one, you can make a stencil by tracing your child's hand on a piece of cardboard. Cut the shape out and trace around it with a sharp knife on the cookie dough to cut the shapes. Also, be aware that smaller hand shapes require less cookie dough and will allow you to make many more cookies from a batch.

Indian Head Bands

You will need:

Large sheets of brown construction paper or brown paper bags

Felt-tip markers or crayons

A stapler

A tape measure

Colored feathers (found at fabric and craft stores)

What to do:

1. Cut the brown paper into strips that are 1½–2 inches wide and you will need to measure each child's head for the length. Make the strip length 2 inches longer than the circumference of the head for securing it to the head.

2. Let the children draw American Indian designs on one side of the paper with the crayons or felt-tip markers.

3. Wrap the headband around the child's head to determine where it will need to be stapled. Remove it from the child's head, holding it in place and staple it.

4. Staple one or more feathers on the back and your little Indian is ready to party!

Leaf Rubbing Placemats

See May Day Festival/Spring Party Craft, Leaf Rubbings.

🎉 GAMES AND 🎉 ACTIVITIES

Hot Corn

You will need:

1 ear of Indian corn
Drum or tin can
Drum stick or a wooden spoon

What to do:

1. Seat all of the children on the ground or floor in a circle. Hand one child the ear of corn.

2. An adult begins beating the drum or tin can. When the beating begins, the children are to pass the ear of Indian corn around the circle in a clockwise direction.

3. When the drum stops beating, the child stuck with the ear of corn is out of the game. If you like, give the child who is out a small bag of candy corn.

4. The game continues in this manner until two children are left. The child who does not get stuck with the ear of corn wins a prize.

Nut Gathering Contest

The American Indian children showed the Pilgrim children where to find nuts, so that they would have plenty to eat during the long winters. You can have a nut gathering at your party, and the great thing about this game is that the children will be helping you clean your yard, while having a great time. We play this game in the fall and tell our children and the neighbor children that the child who finds the most nuts will win a prize. You should see how fast they run to get their buckets from home! We pay all of the children for their help, but give the one who finds the most nuts a prize. Its amazing how fast my yard gets cleaned now! See below for some ideas on how to play this game.

You will need:

A yard with a lot of fallen tree nuts or some purchased unshelled nuts
Children's buckets or heavy paper bags for holding the nuts
Photocopied pictures of squirrels, optional
Paint, optional
Tape, optional

What to do:

1. Before the party, decorate the bags or buckets, by taping the squirrel pictures on them. If desired, paint the children's names onto their bags or buckets. Hide the nuts in your yard.

2. During the party, hand each child their nut holder. At the signal to go, all race like little squirrels to find as many nuts as they can find.

3. Allow the children about 5 minutes to search, then call them all over to an area to sit in a circle.

4. Count each child's nuts out loud to the group. The one who finds the most wins a prize. An appropriate prize would be a

small stuffed squirrel or a bag of peanuts. If the nuts have been purchased, or are edible nuts, then let everyone keep them to take home. If they are not edible, then have the children empty their buckets in a pile. Let them keep the buckets, if using them.

Variation: Have a contest to see who can find the most assortment of nuts, leaves, pinecones, etc.

Turkey Hunt

Make small turkey shapes cut from brown construction paper, photocopied or printed from a computer printer. Hide all of the turkeys either inside or outside of your home. Tell all of the children that they are going turkey hunting, and send them to search for the turkeys on a signal to go. The child to come back with the most turkeys wins.

Animal Archery Contest

At the first Thanksgiving feast, the American Indians demonstrated their skills with the bow and arrow and the Pilgrims demonstrated their musket skills.

You will need:

Animal figures cut from construction paper or printed from a computer: turkey, deer, rabbit, duck and geese

String or rope

Clothespins

A toy bow and arrow set

Pencil and paper

What to do:

1. Before the party, suspend the string or rope up between two trees or poles (between a garage door opening would work well). Attach the animal figures to the string or rope with clothespins.

2. During the party, allow the children 3 shots each to see if they can hit the animal from behind a marked line. How far the marked line should be set back will depend on the bow and arrow set. The child to hit the most animals wins a prize. Write down each child's score after his turn.

Variation: This game may also be played with a regular target, but may need to be played by getting ink on the tip of the arrow to determine where the shot was hit. Since this version can be messy, you may want to play it outdoors or in an area that can be protected from the ink. Another way that you can play this game is to tape each animal shape to a can so that it extends slightly above the can.

Football

For parties with children and adults who are into playing football, consider playing a game in your yard near the end of the party. When playing with young children, use a foam football or a small football. Can you just imagine looking back at holiday pictures years down the road and saying, "Look at Johnny! Do you remember that day when he got walloped by the football! Gee, that sure was a big bruise, wasn't it?"

Blind Luck

You will need:

A large tub of water

1 husked ear of Indian corn (usually found in produce departments in the fall)

Several ears of husked corn

A blindfold: A bandanna or scarf and a clothespin for securing it

What to do:

1. Put all of the corn ears into the tub.

2. Have the children take turns kneeling in front of the tub of water and blindfold them. Move the corn in the tub around to throw them off.

3. The object of the game is to try and pick the piece of Indian corn. Anyone lucky enough to grab it wins a prize. An appropriate prize might be individually wrapped snack bags of candy corn.

Caution: Do not leave children unattended around the tub of water. As soon as the game is over, take the tub away from the party area and empty the water out of the tub. It would be a good idea to have two strong men carry this away. It only takes a second for a small child to fall into it.

Note: Boil the corn after the game and serve it to your guests.

Pumpkin Pie Eating Contest

See Fourth of July Party Game, Pie-Eating Contest. Since pumpkin pie is very filling, only give each child one slice of pie. Some children may not like pumpkin pie, so you may want to have an alternative handy, or just let them cheer the others on. An appropriate prize would be an entire pumpkin pie to take home.

Leaf Pile Treasure Hunt

See Halloween Party. Play this game if you live in a part of the country where there are leaves on the ground in November and not snow.

🎉 FAVOR AND 🎉 PRIZE IDEAS

Candy corn, popcorn balls, boxes of Cracker Jack caramel popcorn, small footballs, inexpensive bow and arrow sets, buckets (see Nut Gathering Contest), miniature pumpkin pies, pumpkin shaped cookies, books about Thanksgiving, sailboats, plastic Indian figures, inexpensive Indian dolls or Indian bead necklaces. See Crafts for the following party favors: Pilgrim Hat Candy Holders, Turkey Placemats, Indian Corn Wreaths, Pinecone Birdfeeders, Corn Husk Dolls, Pinecone Turkeys, Apple Turkeys, Turkey Cookies, Leaf Rubbing Placemats, or Indian Headbands.

Hanukkah Party

• *The 25th day of Kislev* •

Hanukkah (The Festival of Lights) is one of the most important holidays on the Jewish calendar. Hanukkah is the eight-day Jewish festival observing the reconsecration of the Temple in Jerusalem around 165 B.C. by the Jewish family, the Maccabees. The Maccabees resisted the oppression of their nation by the Greek kings of Syria, who forced the Jews to worship the Greek gods. Mattathias Maccabee and his five sons led a revolt that lasted three years and drove the Syrians out. Mattathias died during the first year and never saw the temple regained. There were four major battles against the Syrians before the temple was regained.

The desecrated temple was cleansed and a new altar was built. Then the traditional order of worship was restored. In order for the Jews to rekindle the flame of the Eternal Light they needed pure olive oil. But according to legend, only one day's worth of olive oil could be found. It would be eight days until more oil would arrive at the temple. Miraculously, the one-day supply lasted for eight days and eight nights.

To observe the miracle that happened, Jews light one candle on a menorah each day of the festival. The first evening only one candle is lit, the second two are lit, and so on for the eight days.

The coins given during this festival, known as Hanukkah gelt (money) are a symbol of the Jews' freedom to coin their own money. Many people give gold foil-covered chocolate coins or real coins. Gifts may also be given to one another in celebration of this festival.

🎉 HANUKKAH 🎉
INVITATIONS

Make the invitations in the shape of a dreidel, menorah, or of a Star of

David as shown in illustration (fig. 33). If you like, ask guests to bring a small, wrapped gift to exchange with others. Or, you may choose to give one to each guest as a favor to open.

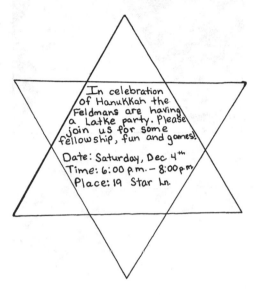

In celebration of Hanukkah the Feldmans are having a Latke party. Please join us for some fellowship, fun and games!

Date: Saturday, Dec 4th
Time: 6:00 p.m. – 8:00 p.m.
Place: 19 Star ln.

Fig. 33. Star of David Invitation

⛵ DECORATIONS ⛵

- Hang yellow and blue balloons and crepe paper from the ceilings. In warm climates, hang them from a mailbox or front porch.

- Cut a Star of David shape from yellow posterboard and write "SHALOM" on it with a blue felt-tip marker. Shalom means "peace" in Hebrew.

- Make a banner that reads "Happy Hanukkah" or "GUT YOM TOV," which means "Happy Holiday" in Yiddish.

- Hang paper-cut chains of the Star of David (see Craft, Star of David Garland).

- Hang homemade or purchased pictures of menorahs, Star of David, dreidels, or gelt (gold foil-covered cardboard circles to resemble coins).

- Place a mezuzah on all of the doorposts of your home.

- Purchase Hanukkah themed tableware, or use a blue tablecloth and yellow and blue tableware.

- Music — The first Hanukkah was celebrated by Judah and his men with "song and harps and lutes, and with cymbals" (I Macc. 4:54). Play Jewish music from different time periods. Play songs such as "Light the Little Candles" or "Dreidel Song."

⛵ FOOD ⛵

Celebrate Hanukkah with friends and family by having a latke party. Serve the following menu items:

- Latkes (potato pancakes)
- Sour cream and applesauce for Latke topping condiments
- Kreplach (dumpling similar to ravioli)
- Salt beef
- Pickles
- Cheese
- Doughnuts (plain or jelly-filled)
- Cider for children and kosher wine for adults

Star of David Cake

You will need:

1 baked 9 × 13-inch caked
2 cans of white frosting
Food coloring: blue and yellow

What to do:

1. Bake and cool the cake as directed. Cut as the illustration shows (fig. 34a).

2. If desired, freeze uncovered for one hour to make frosting spread on easier.

3. Assemble the cake on a foil-covered board as illustrated (fig. 34b).

4. Color 2½ cups of the frosting with the blue food coloring.

5. Attach one small triangle to the each center side of the larger triangle with a little bit of frosting in between to hold it in place.

6. Frost the entire cake with the remaining blue frosting.

7. Color the remaining 1½ cups of frosting with yellow food coloring.

8. Using a frosting bag fitted with a star tip, frost three rows of stars around the top edge of the cake. The rows should appear in the Star of David shape (two triangles with one crossing the other). See illustration (fig. 34c).

9. If desired, add a shell border along the base of the cake with the remaining yellow frosting. Use a frosting bag fitted with a star tip to make the shell border.

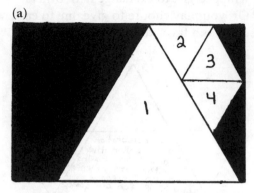

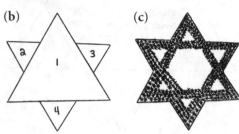

Fig. 34. Star of David Cake

🎉 ARRIVAL 🎉 ACTIVITY

If all of your guests celebrate Hanukkah, gather everyone around and read the story of Judah Maccabee (I Maccabee 4:36-61).

Lighting the Hanukkah Lights

The candles can be lit after sunset. A good time to light them would be just before dinner, with all of your family and friends gathered around. If the children are old enough, allow them to light a candle at least one day.

Just as Hebrew is read from right to left, the candles are placed in the hanukkiah* or menorah beginning at the right side and increasing daily toward the left. The candles are lit using a servant candle called a shammash; the shammash being the taller center candle. The first candle to be lit is the one most recently added. A blessing is said before lighting the candles. The candles should remain lit for at least a half an hour.

♙ CRAFTS ♙

Star of David Garland

Use these paper-cut chains as a craft for guests to make, or make some before the party and use them as decorations.

You will need:

Yellow construction paper cut 4 inches wide and as long as possible
Cardboard stencils in the Star of David shape
Pencils
Scissors

What to do:

1. Fold the strips of paper into an accordion fold (backward then forward and so on). The width of the folds should be slightly smaller than the stencil, so that the stencil slightly overlaps the fold. See illustration (fig. 35a).

2. Trace the stencil shape onto the paper, using a pencil. Make sure that the left and right side of the star overlap the folds or the garland will not turn out. See illustration (fig. 35a).

3. Cut through all of the layers of the paper along the pencil line, making sure that you leave some paper joined at the folds.

4. Unfold the garland to see a string of designs joined together. See illustration (fig. 35b). To create longer strands of garland, tape several strands of garland together on the ends.

5. Hang the strands of garland from walls or china cabinets.

Variation: You can also make these in menorah or dreidel shapes, but the Star of David works best.

(a)

(b)

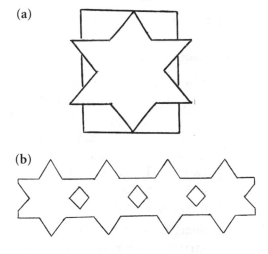

Fig. 35. Star of David Garland

A hanukkiah is a nine-branched Jewish candelabra used during Hanukkah.

Gelt Baskets

See May Day Festival/Spring Party Craft, May Day Basket. Use blue construction paper to make the baskets. Decorate the baskets with yellow or gold metallic trim. Decorate the sides of the baskets with Star of David shapes made from glued on yellow yarn or construction paper triangles. You can even use the gold-foil wrappers from chocolate coins to decorate the basket. Cut out circle coin shapes and glue or tape them onto the sides of the basket.

Egg Carton Dreidel Toy

You will need:

Egg cartons
Wood dowels or meat skewers
Glue
Pencil sharpeners
Felt-tip markers or acrylic paint

What to do:

1. Cut the dowels or meat skewers to a length appropriate to the depth of the egg carton. The handle should extend about 1½ inches above the edge of the carton. The point should be about a ½ inch below the carton. See illustration (fig. 36).

2. Sharpen the dowel tip, if necessary, with a pencil sharpener or a pocket knife. If using a meat skewer, it may already have a pointed end.

3. Cut the egg carton into sections. Use one section per dreidel.

4. Paint or draw on the four sides of the dreidel as described under Dreidel Game.

Fig. 36. Egg Carton Dreidel Toy

Star of David Picture Frames

You will need:

Paper tablecloth or newspaper
Popsicle sticks, 6 per guests
Glue
Felt-tip markers
Polaroid camera or a digital camera (something that can give instant pictures)
Self adhesive backed magnets (found in hardware and craft stores)
Scissors

What to do:

1. Cover a table or work area with the tablecloth or newspaper to protect it.

2. Have guests glue together a tri-

angle shape using three popsicle sticks. Place the glue on just the ends of the popsicle sticks. Have each child make two of these triangle shapes.

3. Glue the two triangle shapes together into a Star of David shape. Write each guest's name on his frame and set in a safe place until the glue has dried.

4. Meanwhile, take a photo of each guest for the frames, and play some games until the star shaped frames dry.

5. Once the frames are dry, cut the photos into hexagon shapes to fit the center of each star that it goes with. Glue the photo to the frame.

6. Cut pieces of self-adhesive magnets to the size of the popsicle sticks and stick to the back of the frame. You now have a picture frame ready to be hung on a refrigerator door!

Paper Snowflakes

You will need:

White paper, a few pieces per guest
Scissors, 1 pair per guest, if possible
A bowl or cup for tracing
Pencils

What to do:

1. Trace a circle on a piece of paper, using the bowl or cup, and cut out the circle shape.

2. Fold the circle in half, and then fold it three more times, until the folded piece looks like a slice of pizza.

3. Cut into the folds making various types of cuts. Make some half round cuts, some triangle cuts, some square, etc. Tell everyone to get creative.

4. Unfold the paper and see how unique and different everyone's snowflakes are. Help anyone having trouble and show him the correct way to do it. They will soon catch on. Tell everyone to hang these on their windows at home.

Make Candles

Buy a candle making kit at a craft store and make candles for a menorah with your guests.

🎉 GAMES AND 🎉 ACTIVITIES

Play Traditional Games

Bring out a chess game or a deck of cards and play them.

Dreidel Game

The most popular game played during Hanukkah is played with a spinning top called a dreidel. The letters found on the dreidels four sides are נ (nun), ג (gimel), ה (he), ש (shin). They stand for Yiddish words meaning "take" (nem) or "nothing" (nisht), "give" (gib) or "all" (gantz), "half" (halb), and "put" (shetl). Spin a dreidel while singing the "Dreidel Song." Use Hanukkah gelt when playing with the dreidel. The letters indicate the penalties of the game. The letters are also interpreted to stand for the phrase nes gadol haya sham ("a great miracle happened there"). The game is played for enjoyment and as a reminder of the Hanukkah story.

What to do:

1. Each player contributes an agreed-upon amount of gold foil-covered chocolate coins, candy or nuts into a kitty.

2. Each player takes a turn spinning the dreidel. The following are the rules for each of the following spins:

   • Nun — nothing happens and the player passes.

   • Gimel — the player gets everything in the kitty and everyone must re-contribute the agreed amount to the kitty.

   • He — the player gets half of the kitty.

   • Shin — the player must put into the kitty whatever forfeit has been agreed upon before the game.

3. The game ends when one player has won everything from the others or when all decide to stop (the winner being the player who wins the most).

Variation: The letters may represent a numerical value: nun = 50; gimel = 3; he = 5; shin = 300. The players write the score down on a pad of paper. Play a set amount of rounds. The player with the highest score wins.

Pin the Shammash on the Menorah

You will need:

A blue piece of posterboard
Yellow and red construction paper
Scissors
Glue
Tape
Blindfold (a scarf or bandanna) and a clothespin for attaching

What to do:

1. Before the party, cut a nine-branched menorah shape out of the yellow paper and glue it the blue posterboard. Hang the posterboard on a wall, door or refrigerator.

2. Cut candle shapes out of the red paper. Cut 1 candle shape for every player and write a player's name on his candle.

3. During the party, put a loop of tape on the backside of each candle.

4. Line the players up in a line in front of the menorah and give each child his paper candle.

5. Blindfold the first child in line.

6. Gently spin him around three times, stopping in front of the menorah.

7. He must then try to "pin" the candle or "shammash" on the menorah. Each child takes a turn. The child who comes the closest to the center branch on the menorah wins.

Shammash Relay

You will need:

- 2 empty toilet paper tubes as a shammash
- 2 pretend or real menorahs

What to do:

1. Divide the children into two equal groups and stand them in line behind a marked starting line.
2. Set the menorahs on a table about 20 feet away from the starting line.
3. On the signal to go, the first two children in each line run to the menorah and pretend to light it, then run back, pass the toilet paper tube off to the next child in line who then does the same. This continues on until the first team to have all of its players finish first wins.

Latke Flipping Relay

You will need:

- 2 spatulas
- 2 beanbags or zippered plastic bags filled with dried lentil beans

What to do:

1. Divide the children into two equal teams and stand them behind a starting line.
2. Mark a goal about 15–20 feet away.
3. Hand the first child in each line a spatula and a beanbag or filled plastic bag.
4. At the signal to go, they must put their "latke" on top of their spatula, run to the goal, flip their latke onto their spatula, pick it up if it drops, replace it back onto the spatula, and race back to their team.
5. They pass the spatula and latke to the next child in line, who then does the same as the first. This continues on until the first team has each member complete the task. The first team to finish wins. An appropriate prize would be an inexpensive spatula for each player on the winning team.

🎉 FAVOR AND 🎉 PRIZE IDEAS

Items with the Star of David or menorahs on them (lapel pins, toys, stickers, pencils, erasers, tins full of candy, or cookies, etc.), Hanukkah gelt (coins or gold foil-covered chocolate coins), dreidels, religious necklaces, candle holders, Star of David Garland (see Crafts), Gelt Baskets (see Crafts), Egg Carton Dreidel Toy (see Crafts), Star of David Picture Frames (see Crafts), Paper Snowflakes (see Crafts), or spatulas (see Games and Activities, Latke Flipping Relay).

Christmas Party

• *December 25* •

Christmas is the holiday when Christians celebrate the story of the birth of Jesus. The holiday was originally celebrated on January 6, the Feast of the Epiphany. This feast was changed to offset pagan sun ceremonies that celebrated the winter solstice.

There is just something about the Christmas season that wakes up all of my senses, and brings back great memories and feelings for me. Ahh … the smell of fresh cut pine trees and cookies baking in the oven. The anticipation felt when the mail person arrives with bundled packages of goodies and letters coming in everyday from old friends and family members. Christmas parties for children with yummy goodies and caroling. Christmas is such a fun season. Why not add to that special excitement by having a party with the season in mind? Gather up your friends and relatives and take advantage of the endless theme possibilities that the season offers. Because there are so many good craft ideas for this sea-

son, this party has an abundance of them to choose from. You can use the ideas listed in this chapter for so many things, such as school class parties, family holiday get togethers, church parties, neighborhood parties, Santa's workshop parties, etc. However you choose to use these ideas, I'm sure that everyone will enjoy experiencing the true meaning of Christmas with them. Merry Christmas!

🎉 CHRISTMAS 🎉 TREE INVITATION

Trace a tree shape on green paper as the one illustrated (fig. 37a & b), using a stencil or a cookie cutter for tracing the shape. Cut the shape out and write your message as shown (fig. 37a & b). Put a star sticker at the top of the tree. Cut out little round circles

156

from colored paper, using a hole puncher and glue them to the front of the tree. Try to keep in mind that not all of your guests may celebrate Christmas. If that is the case with your child's friends, you could instead keep your invitation theme more of a winter theme. Have your child find out, if possible, whether or not his friends celebrate Christmas. Many office supply stores sell great winter theme computer paper. You could write a universal message on the invitation that would appeal to all of your guests. Make any necessary changes in your party theme to make the invited child feel comfortable. Try not to schedule your party too close to Christmas Day, since it may be hectic for many families.

🎉 DECORATIONS 🎉

One of the great things about having a party at this time of the year is that your home is probably already decorated for this holiday, so only a few more things may even be necessary.

- If you live in a part of the country where there isn't much snow or cold weather, put red and green crepe paper and balloons on the mailbox, front porch and in the party area.

- Decorate your house with the usual Christmas decorations; a wreath on the front door, garland on the railings and fireplace mantels, a decorated Christmas tree with the lights turned on, mistletoe hanging in a doorway, paper chains (see Crafts, Paper Chains), etc. If your party is

(a)

(b)

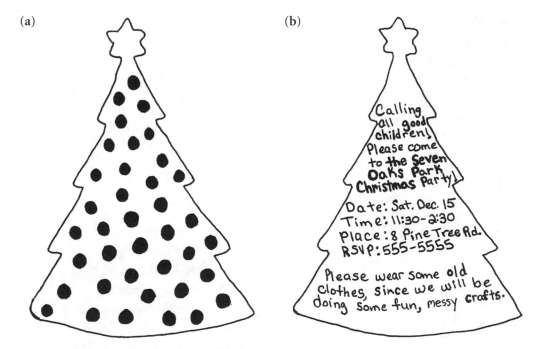

Fig. 37. Christmas Tree Invitation

during the evening, turn on outside Christmas lights.

- Make a sign that reads "Caution Reindeer Crossing." Paint reindeer-type tracks on the sign or paint a picture of Rudolph the Red-Nosed Reindeer.

- Use a Christmas tablecloth and tableware or use a red tablecloth and green tableware. Let your child cut out little Christmas tree shapes and tape them to the tablecloth.

- Make a lollipop tree with a green foam cone (found at craft stores). Stick lollipops all around the cone.

- Have Christmas music playing indoors as the guests arrive. Play upbeat children's Christmas songs like "Rudolph the Red-Nosed Reindeer" (Gene Autry), "Santa Claus Is Coming to Town" (Gene Autry), "Jingle Bells" (Jim Reeves), "Frosty the Snowman" (Patti Page), or "Feliz Navidad" (José Feliciano).

- Ask a friend or relative to dress as Santa and come to your home with his Santa sack full of wrapped party favors to pass out to the children.

- If an adult can always be nearby to watch little hands, light a fire in the fireplace.

♣ FOOD ♣

Since this season will most likely be a busy one for you, serve something simple for a casual party.

- Warm bowls of soup, chili, gumbo, or stew

- Cheese and crackers or crusty French bread rolls

–or–

- A tray of deli meats and cheeses
- Sliced bread
- Christmas cookies
- Hot cocoa or hot spiced apple cider
- Snacks: popcorn, roasted chestnuts, Christmas candy
- Find Christmas theme popsicles (e.g., green trees) to serve with the cake for simplicity

Cake

In Canada, French-speaking families end the holiday season with a feast on January 6. A special fruitcake is baked with a dried bean and a dried pea in it. The boy and girl who find these surprises in their pieces of cake are named the King and Queen of the Twelfth Night. If desired, serve your cake with a hidden bean and a pea in it, or hide 2 jellybeans. To hide jellybeans, cut a slit in the cake after baking and insert them before frosting the cake. Award prizes to the children who find the hidden surprises.

Candy Cane Cake

You will need:

1 baked 9 × 13-inch cake

4 cups of white frosting

Green food coloring

¼–¾ cup of red frosting

Red maraschino cherry halves, optional

Rose or green colored cellophane wrap, optional

What to do:

1. Bake and cool cake as directed. Cut the cake as shown in illustration (fig. 38a). If desired, freeze uncovered for about one hour to make frosting spread easier.

2. Cover a board that is about 15 × 24 inches with aluminum foil. If desired, cover the foil with the rose or green colored cellophane to give a unique appearance.

3. Remove the cake from the freezer and arrange on covered board as shown in illustration (fig. 38b).

4. Frost the entire cake with white frosting, reserving about 1 cup for decorating.

5. Color about 1 cup of frosting with green food coloring. Using a decorator's bag fitted with a star tip or a rose tip, pipe green frosting stripes onto the cake on the diagonal. Pipe a green shell border along the bottom edge of the cake.

6. Using a frosting bag fitted with a small round tip frost a red stripe on each side of the green stripes. If not using the maraschino cherries, switch the frosting tip to a star tip or a rose tip, and pipe wider red stripes on the cake. If using the maraschino cherry halves, place them on the cake diagonally to make stripes.

Variation: Use red and green colored sugar for stripes.

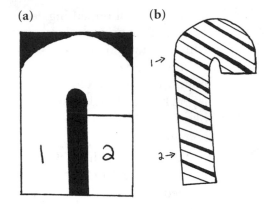

(a)   **(b)**

Fig. 38. Candy Cane Cake

Santa Claus Cake

You will need:

1 baked heart shaped cake

4–5 cups of icing, the amount will depend on the size of the cake pan

Red food coloring

2 blue jellybeans or other similar sized candy

What to do:

1. Bake and cool the cake as directed. If desired, freeze the cake uncovered for one hour to make the frosting spread on the cake easier.

2. Frost the face white as illustrated (fig. 39), leaving the top ⅓ (the pointed end) of the cake unfrosted. Reserve about 1–1½ cups of white frosting and set aside.

3. Color the remaining frosting with red food coloring and frost the Santa hat on the top ⅓ (the pointed end) of the cake. Frost a round red nose on the center of the face.

4. Using a frosting bag fitted with

a star tip for all remaining decorating, frost on a swirled white frosting circle at the point of the hat for a pom-pom. The swirl should be two layers high and look kind of like a swirl of soft custard ice cream.

5. At the edge of the hat, where it meets the face, frost on a swirled hat rim.

6. Put on the two jellybeans for the eyes.

7. Above the eyes, frost two straight white lines with the frosting bag, for the eyebrows.

8. Below the nose, frost a mustache, using the frosting bag.

9. For the beard, just frost rows of stars with the white frosting. See illustration (fig. 39).

Fig. 39. Santa Cake

Santa Claus Cupcakes

You will need:

Baked cupcakes
3 cups white frosting
Red and yellow food coloring
Red colored sugar
Miniature white marshmallows
Chocolate chips or M & M's candies
Maraschino cherries

What to do:

1. Bake and cool cupcakes as directed. Color 2 cups of frosting a light flesh color by adding a little yellow and red food coloring. Frost the tops of cupcakes flesh colored.

2. Sprinkle the top $\frac{1}{3}$ of the cupcake with red sugar, for the cap.

3. Place a miniature marshmallow on one end of the cap for a tassel.

4. Press two chocolate chips in, pointed side down for the eyes, or use the M & M's candies for eyes.

5. Use a maraschino cherry half for the nose.

6. Place the remaining white frosting in a decorator's bag fitted with a small round tip. Pipe frosting swirls on the

Fig. 40. Santa Claus Cupcakes

lower half of the cupcake for a beard.

7. If desired, use red M & M's for rosy cheeks. See illustration (fig. 40).

🎉 ARRIVAL 🎉 OF GUESTS

In Spain, Puerto Rico, Mexico, and throughout Central and South America, families display mangers scenes called nacimientos or presepios. The figure of the baby Jesus is not added until Christmas Eve. The three Kings are said to bring gifts to children on January 6. The children leave their shoes on the windowsill at night filled with carrots, barley, or straw for the camels of the Three Kings, in hopes that they will find them filled in the morning with goodies. Tell your guests to leave their shoes at the door upon entering, and tell them when they leave they will find them filled with goodies. Have a helper sneak to fill them later during the party, while the children aren't looking.

Holiday Air Freshener

An hour or so before your guests arrive, simmer a pot of the following ingredients on the stove to give your home a wonderful holiday aroma!

10 whole cloves
1 cinnamon stick or 1 tsp. ground cinnamon
1 tsp. nutmeg

1 tsp. allspice
1 tsp. ginger

What to do:

1. Fill a small saucepan half-full with water and add all of the above spices. Stir to mix.

2. Bring to a boil over medium heat. Reduce heat and simmer for about 45 minutes.

3. Remove from heat and just set the saucepan on a back burner to cool down.

🎉 CRAFTS 🎉

During the holiday season, sometimes we forget to slow down and take it easy. Take time out of your busy schedule, even if just for one afternoon, to sit down with your family and make a craft together. Turn on some holiday tunes and relax. Perhaps your child could give one of these crafts to a family member, a friend, or even a needy family for Christmas.

Angels on High

Make these heavenly little angels as party favors for your guests to take home and hang on their tree, or let them take them apart and eat them.

You will need:

7 × 7-inch square of white material, 1 per guest
6 × 6-inch square of lacy white fabric or tulle, 1 per guest
Wrapped ball-shaped suckers, 1 per guest

White yarn

Gold ribbon or yellow yarn (17 inches long per angel)

Gold thread (about 4 inches per angel)

Scissors

Glue

Yellow felt

Craft wiggle eyes (5mm or larger and found in craft stores), 2 per guest

Red felt-tip marker

What to do:

1. Wrap a square of white material around the top of one sucker. Tie the material in place with the white yarn just below the sucker ball.

2. Wrap the lace fabric or tulle around the sucker stick just slightly above the ball of the sucker. As you wrap the lace or tulle around, gather it together just below the ball of the sucker.

3. Tie the lace or tulle in place with the gold ribbon or yellow yarn, just below the ball of the sucker as shown in illustration (fig. 41).

4. Slightly fan out the lace fabric or tulle at the top and bottom.

5. Loop and tie a piece of gold thread into a halo and glue it to the back of the "angel's head."

6. Cut a pair of wings from the yellow felt and glue them to the back of the angel.

7. Glue the eyes in place and draw on a red mouth.

Fig. 41. Angels on High

Glitter Ball Ornaments

You will need:

Foam balls about 3 inches in diameter (found at craft stores)

Colored glitter in a few colors (found at craft stores)

White glue

A plastic disposable bowl

Paint brushes

Pipe cleaners

Old shoeboxes or shirt boxes

Newspaper

Labeled paper bags, 1 per child

What to do:

1. Place the glitter in shoeboxes or shirt boxes, and set on a table that is covered with newspaper. Use one box for each color. Pour some glue into the disposable bowl and set on the newspaper. Place the other items on the newspaper.

2. Let the children paint some glue onto one section of a foam ball. Then place the ball over the box of glitter and pour some glitter over the glue. Continue doing sections with the glue and the glitter until the entire ball is covered. Allow the ball to dry.

3. Punch a hole in the top of the ball. Put some glue onto the end of a pipe cleaner and place in the hole. Bend a hook on the other end to use as a hanger. Place in a bag labeled with the child's name.

Variation: Use glass ball ornaments, and let the children write their names on the balls with the glue, then pour the glitter over the glue.

Variation: Make pinecone ornaments using this method, by replacing pinecones with foam balls.

Salt Dough Ornaments

The tradition of making salt dough is a very old one. The classical Egyptians, Greeks and Romans paid homage to their gods by making offerings of dough figures. During the 19th century, Germans made ornaments of dough for their Christmas trees. They later added especially large amounts of salt to make the ornaments less appealing to mice and other vermin.

These ornaments must be made at the beginning of the party to allow enough time for making, baking, cooling and decorating. In order for the children to have plenty of time to finish these, at least a 3-hour party would be required. See above to make this classic Christmas ornament.

You will need:

2 cups flour

1 cup salt

1 tbsp. olive oil

1 cup of water

Toothpicks

Garlic press

Straws or metal paper clips (do not use paper clips with a plastic coating)

Beads for eyes, optional

Glue, optional

Clear gloss finish or glaze

A small box or a piece of cardboard, 1 per guest

What to do:

1. Make the dough before the party. Mix salt, oil and water. Then mix in flour. Knead together. The dough *must* be kneaded or it will crack during baking. Add more water, flour or salt, if necessary, to make dough more workable. Store in an airtight plastic container or a zippered plastic bag in the refrigerator until needed.

2. When guests arrive, roll or pat the dough so that it is flat enough to be cut with cookie cutters, or have the children shape it into desired shapes or figures. Remember though, that the thicker the shapes the longer it will take them to bake. It would be best to keep them on the thin side. Use a toothpick to add features to the creations. Use the garlic press to create hair or grass, by pushing the dough through it and

cutting it off. It may be necessary to use a dab of water to make hair, grass or other objects stick on.

3. Punch a hole in the top of each ornament for hanging, using a straw, or push a paper clip into the top of the ornament leaving about ¼ inch exposed for a hanger.

4. To help prevent cracking when baking, smooth the dough edges with wet fingertips. Bake at 325° for about one hour and cook thin shapes for ½ hour, or until hard. Cool on a wire rack.

5. Remove from the oven and cool for one hour.

6. Paint with acrylic paint or poster paint. If desired, glue on beads for eyes.

7. Seal with clear gloss finish or glaze (found in craft stores). Since the ornaments may still be wet, set them in a small box or on top of a piece of cardboard so that the children may safely take the ornaments home.

Variation: If desired, add food coloring to the water before adding flour and make a few batches of different colors.

Paper Chains

These festive decorations are fun and very easy to make.

You will need:

Various colors of construction paper or shiny metallic origami paper

Scissors
Transparent tape or stapler

What to do:

1. Before the party, cut a lot of strips so that you won't need to mess with it during the party. If using the construction paper, cut ¾-inch wide × 6-inch long strips. If using the origami paper, cut 1½ × 6-inch strips, and fold the long edges to the center of the strip, overlapping them slightly to hide the appearance of the white backing on the paper.

2. During the party, let the children assemble the chains. Connect the two ends of one strip with a piece of tape or staple to create the first ring. If using the origami paper, make sure that the fold is facing in.

3. Make a second ring by looping it through the first ring, and again tape or staple the ends. Continue linking strips, alternating colors, until you have a long chain to deck the halls! Tell the children to decorate their Christmas tree, a window, a china cabinet, or their room with these.

Popcorn Garland

You will need:

A large amount of plain popcorn (some will be eaten)
Plastic needles, 1 per child (if using real needles, use them where you can easily find them if they fall)
Thread

Scissors

Buttons, 2 per child

Labeled paper bags, 1 per child

What to do:

1. Thread the needle, doubling the thread, and tie a few knots at the end.

2. Slip a button on the thread and let it drop to the knot.

3. Once the button is in place, begin threading the popcorn one piece at a time by piercing it with the threaded needle. Slide the piece of popcorn down the thread until it meets the button. Continue threading popcorn until you have either run out of room on the thread or it is at the desired length.

4. Place another button on the opposite end and tie a knot to keep the button and the popcorn in place. Tell the children to hang the garland on their Christmas tree when they get it home and place it in a bag labeled with their name.

Reindeer Candy Canes

These make for great party favors for neighborhood parties, school parties, church parties, etc. If you like, make them before the party, or let the children make one for themselves.

You will need:

Peppermint candy canes (standard size), 1 per child

Brown pipe cleaners (6mm × 12 inches), 1 per child

Small wiggle eyes (7mm or smaller and found in craft stores), 2 per child

Tiny red pompoms (¼ inch or smaller and found in craft stores), 1 per child

Glue

What to do:

1. Keep the plastic on the candy cane to protect it from the glue. Wrap one brown pipe cleaner around the top of a candy cane, twisting it around once, and turning the ends up to look like half of a square. If you like, get creative and bend it to look more realistic. The pipe cleaner should resemble reindeer antlers.

2. Glue a small red pompom on the lower end of the crook of the candy cane to look like Rudolph's red nose.

3. Glue two eyes about 1 inch above the nose. The children can decorate their Christmas trees with these or gobble them up!

Beaded Candy Cane Ornaments

You will need:

Three 10-inch pieces of wire (use 20 or 24 gauge galvanized wire)

Wire cutters (if your wire doesn't come with a cutter)

Needle nose pliers

30 6mm crystal beads of each color; red, white and green

3 bowls

What to do:

1. Before the party, pre-cut the wire into 10-inch pieces. With needle nose pliers, bend the wire, making a very small loop on one end of each piece of wire (this will keep the beads from falling off of the wire).

2. The day of the party, put all of the beads in bowls of each separate color and place on a table.

3. Seat each child at the table with 3 pieces of wire and tell them to string one wire with red beads, one with white beads and one with green beads.

4. When they have finished putting the beads on all of their wires, help them put another small loop on the end of each strand to hold on all of the beads.

5. Have them put all of the 3 strands together, making them even. Ask them to twist the strands together, then bend at the top, like a candy cane. They are now ready to be hung on a tree!

Beaded Ball Ornaments

You will need:

Round white foam balls about 3 inches in diameter (found in craft stores)

Straight pins with a round tip (check the size to be sure your bead hole is not larger than your pinhead)

Long decorative straight pins with a bead on the end (found at fabric stores)

Colorful 6mm beads

Colorful sequins, optional

Ribbon

What to do:

1. Arrange this craft in an area with a smooth floor, so that if a pin should fall to the ground it can be easily found. Let the children thread a bead and then a sequin onto a straight pin. Push the pointed end of the straight pin into the foam ball. Repeat with more beaded pins until the ball is completely covered.

2. Tie a ribbon into a pretty bow. Push the long straight pin through the bow and into the foam ball for a hanger. Tell the children to hang these beautiful ornaments on their Christmas trees at home.

Gingerbread Houses

You will need:

2 large eggs

3½ cups of sifted powdered sugar

½ teaspoon cream of tartar

Plastic zippered sandwich bags, 1 per child

Half-pint milk or cream cartons, 1 per child

Foam dinner size plates or cardboard squares, 1 per child

Graham cracker squares, 6 per child

Assorted candies: candy canes, gumdrops, green mint candy leaves, peppermint pinwheels, licorice, etc.

Bowls

Vanilla Vienna finger sandwich
cookies cut in half at the center

Scissors

What to do:

1. Before the party, make the decorator frosting. Separate the
   egg whites from the 2 eggs. Put
   the egg whites in a mixing bowl
   and mix with a mixer. Beat the
   egg whites until they form stiff
   peaks when you lift the beaters.
   Gradually add sifted powdered
   sugar and cream of tartar. Beat
   until stiff. Spoon some frosting
   into each sandwich bag and
   seal shut. Refrigerate until
   needed.

2. Rinse out the milk or cream
   cartons and let them dry. Staple
   the spout closed.

3. During the party, place the candies in individual bowls and set
   them on a table that is covered
   with a paper tablecloth or
   newspaper. Snip off a small
   corner of each frosting bag and
   give one to each child. Also,
   give each child a foam plate or
   piece of cardboard with a milk
   or cream carton on it.

4. Trim 4 graham cracker squares,
   if necessary, to make them fit
   on the sides of the carton.
   Squeeze a layer of frosting onto
   1 graham cracker. Press it onto
   one side of the carton. Repeat
   on all sides.

5. Squeeze a thick layer of frosting onto one side of 2 graham
   cracker squares. Press them
   onto the top of the carton to
   make the roof.

6. Use the frosting bags to
   squeeze frosting on any exposed parts of the carton. Stick
   the candies to the frosting to
   decorate the house. Use more
   frosting to decorate as desired.
   Attach a Vienna finger cookie
   half with frosting to make a
   door for the house. Press mint
   candy leaves next to the door to
   resemble bushes.

Caution: Remind the children that
the frosting has raw eggs in it, and that
it is good for gluing, but not for eating.
It may make them sick. They may eat
some of the candy before the frosting
touches it though.

Variation: If you like, pre-assem-
ble the gingerbread houses before the
party and let the children decorate
them with them frosting. Also, double
or triple the frosting recipe if you will
be having a lot of guests. Each child
should have a bag full of frosting.

Clothespin Reindeer Ornaments

The clothespins used for these ornaments can usually be found in craft
stores during the holiday season. Purchase the old fashioned type of clothespins that do not have a wire spring. See
illustration (fig. 42).

You will need:

Wooden clothespins with flat sides, 2
   per ornament

Brown wood stain

Gold ribbon

Hot glue (only to be used by an
   adult)

Ordinary craft glue

Tiny red pompoms, 1 per ornament

Wiggle eyes, 5–7 mm (depending on the size of the clothespin), 2 per ornament

What to do:

1. Before the party, stain all sides of the clothespins and allow them to dry.

2. Hot glue the two clothespins together, with a loop of gold ribbon sandwiched in between them for a hanger. One clothespin should face up and the other should face down, and one round end should be over the other, as illustrated (fig. 42). Allow clothespins to dry.

3. During the party, show the children an example of a finished Clothespin Reindeer

Fig. 42. Clothespin Reindeer Ornament

Ornament to help them understand what to do.

4. Have them glue on two wiggle eyes and a red pompom nose.

Popsicle Stick Reindeer Ornaments

You will need:

Wooden popsicle sticks, 3 per ornament

Brown wood stain

Metal Christmas ornament hooks, 1 per ornament

Green ribbon

⅜-inch wiggle eyes, 2 per ornament

½-inch red pompoms

Glue

What to do:

1. Before the day of the party, stain the popsicle sticks and allow them to dry.

2. During the party, have the children wrap a metal ornament hook around the center of one popsicle stick and attach a bow of ribbon to the hook.

3. Have them glue three popsicle sticks together as illustrated (fig. 43).

4. Glue a red pompom at the pointed end for a nose.

5. Glue the two wiggle eyes in place. You ornament is now ready for hanging!

Advent Trees

Cut out Christmas tree shapes from green construction paper. Cut out

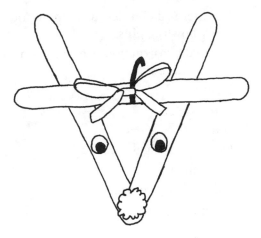

Fig. 43. Popsicle Stick Reindeer Ornament

little circle shapes from colored construction paper, using a hole puncher. Cut out one little circle for each day left until Christmas from the day of the party. Stick a star sticker on the top of the tree. Place the tree and the little circles in a zippered plastic bag with a note thanking your guests for coming to the party and instructions to glue one circle on the tree every day until Christmas. When they have their last "ornament" on the tree IT IS CHRISTMAS!!! If you like, have the children cut out these themselves and put them in labeled bags.

☖ GAMES AND ☖ ACTIVITIES

Reindeer Hunt

You will need:

Several reindeer shapes made of brown construction paper or printed from a computer

1 Rudolph reindeer with a red nose
Jingle bells

What to do:

1. Before the party, hide the reindeer all over the inside of house (outdoors in warm climates).

2. Tell the children that Santa can't find his reindeer and that they must help him find them. At the signal to go (the ringing of the jingle bells), the children search for Santa's reindeer. The one to find Rudolph and the one to find the most reindeer wins a prize. An appropriate prize would be a Reindeer Candy Cane or a book about Rudolph the Red-Nosed Reindeer.

Pin the Star on Top of the Christmas Tree

You will need:

A Christmas tree made out of green construction paper
One yellow paper star for each guest
Tape
Blindfold (a bandanna or scarf) with a clothespin for easy placement

What to do:

1. Before the party, write the children's names on the front of their stars. Hang the tree up on a wall, door or refrigerator.

2. During the party, put a loop of tape on the back of each star and pass them out to the children.

3. Line the children up single file. Blindfold the first child in line and gently spin him around a few times stopping him in front of the tree. He must try to "pin" the star on top of the tree. Continue with the other children. The child to pin the star the closest to the top of the tree wins.

Santa's Sack

You will need:

1 wrapped prize per guest
Pillowcase
Christmas music

What to do:

1. Fill the pillowcase full of the wrapped presents and seat all of the children in a circle on the floor.

2. Hand the "Santa sack" to one child. When the music begins, the children all pass Santa's sack around the circle clockwise.

3. When the music stops, the child holding the sack takes out a present and is then out of the game. He may go off to the side and open his gift.

4. Begin the music again and continue until only one child remains. He receives the last gift and a prize.

Reindeer Bowling

You will need:

6 empty plastic ½-gallon milk containers, juice containers, plastic 2-liter soda bottles, or even plastic toy bowling pins
Colored construction paper: brown, tan and red
Scissors
Tape
Glue
Large craft wiggle eyes
Red ball
Black felt-tip marker
Paper and pencil

What to do:

1. Before the party, wrap the brown paper around the plastic bottles to create the reindeer body and tape in place. If using the bowling pins, this step really isn't necessary. See illustration for bowling pin option (fig. 44).

2. Make two oval-shaped ears from the brown paper. Make two small oval shapes from the tan paper and glue one to each brown oval shape, to create the insides of the ears. Glue a set of ears to the top of each bottle, sticking out away from the bottle.

3. Cut a large oval shape from the tan paper and glue it onto each "body" to create the reindeer's tummy.

4. Glue or tape a set of wiggle eyes onto each reindeer. Draw on a black, round nose for all but one reindeer. Cut a large round nose from the red paper for Rudolph and glue onto one bottle. Draw on a mouth and facial features for each reindeer.

5. During the party, set up the "reindeer" on the floor or ground as you would bowling pins, in a triangle formation (a garage or basement floor makes a good alley). Place the Rudolph bottle in the front. Allow the children to take turns rolling the ball at the pins. Each child gets two rolls of the ball. Record each child's score after they are finished with their turn. The one to knock the most pins down wins. Be prepared with plenty of inexpensive prizes (e.g., Christmas candy), as they may all win.

Fig. 44. Reindeer Bowling Pin

Chimney Toss

You will need:

3 foam balls (found in craft stores)

Large cardboard box

Red and black paint (plus any other colors desired)

Craft knife or scissors

What to do:

1. Before the party, cut a hole out of the front of the box to resemble a chimney opening. Cut the hole about 9–12 inches wide, or large enough for the foam balls to fit through without too much trouble.

2. Paint the box red and paint black rectangle squares on it to resemble bricks. If desired, paint a mantel with stockings hanging from it and maybe a clock on top.

3. During the party, line the children up to take turns tossing the "snowballs" into the chimney opening. Each child gets 3 tosses. The child to get the most balls into the hole wins.

Variation: Rolls of brick-looking corrugated cardboard can be purchased during the Christmas season at paper supply stores and teachers' supply stores. You can staple the roll around the cardboard box, instead of painting it. If you like, leave an area open at the top of the chimney for the children to throw the "snowballs" into the top of the chimney instead of the front.

Christmas Candy Guess

Fill a candy jar (preferably one shaped like a Christmas tree) with red and green M & M's. Count the candy pieces as you place them in the jar. Write the number on a small piece of paper, fold it up, and tape it to the bottom of the jar. During the party, give everyone a slip of paper and a pencil and tell them to write down what they guess is the correct amount of candy in the jar. The child to guess the closest wins the jar of M & M's.

Story Time

If all of your guests celebrate Christmas, read the story of the birth of Jesus from a children's book, complete with colored pictures. Or you could read the books "The Night Before Christmas," "Rudolph the Red Nosed Reindeer," or even "Frosty the Snowman."

Sing Christmas Carols

Nothing relieves stress like a song. If an adult can always be nearby to watch little hands, light a fire in the fireplace and sing Christmas carols by it. Provide song sheets for everyone and ask a friend or relative who is musically talented to play an instrument, such as a guitar. If you have a piano, sing carols around it.

Now that everyone has had a little practice at singing, share the holiday spirit by inviting everyone to join you in caroling around the neighborhood, at an area hospital, or even an elderly home. Remind everyone that it's not how well you sing that counts, but it's the smile that you put behind the music that does! Spread the joy!

Shoe Relay

In France, children put their shoes by the fireplace for Père Nöel to fill with gifts on December 24. If you live in an area where it is too cold to play

this game outdoors, play it in a basement or a large open area. This game could be played at the very beginning of the party (see Arrival of Guests), or instead of the arrival activity.

What to do:

1. Divide the children into two equal teams and line them up behind a marked starting line. Set a goal at the other end of the basement or room.

2. At the signal to go, the first child in line runs to the goal, removes his shoes and runs back to touch off the next child in line, who must do the same. The game continues in this manner until the first team has all of its players complete the task. They are the winners.

Snowball Fight

You will need:

White crumpled paper or white foam balls as snowball ammunition

Two long ropes or pieces of string of equal length

A stopwatch or kitchen timer

What to do:

1. Place the ropes on the ground or floor, parallel to one another. They should be 8–10 feet apart.

2. Divide the children into two equal teams and have them stand behind their string.

3. Give each child a crumpled ball of paper or a foam ball. On the signal to go, start the timer for

one minute. All players must try to throw their "snowball" across the other team's rope without crossing their team's rope. They all continue throwing the balls again and again until one minute is up.

4. When the timer goes off or the minute is up, have everyone stop and count the "snowballs" on their side of the rope. Any snowballs in the center and not behind the rope are not counted. The team with the least amount of snowballs wins.

Christmas Piñata

In Mexico, piñatas are filled with candy, oranges and peanuts at Christmas time. You can have one too, but you may want to skip the oranges. Piñatas can be purchased in the shape of Christmas trees or Santa Claus during the holiday season, or see the Holiday Piñata chapter of this book to see how to make a piñata. If the weather in your area won't allow you to hang your piñata outdoors, hang it in a basement or a garage.

🎩 FAVOR AND 🎩 PRIZE IDEAS

Christmas theme items (e.g., lapel pins, stickers, pencils, erasers, etc.), jingle bell necklaces, Christmas candy, small filled stockings, Santa hats, small tins full of homemade fudge or cookies, Christmas cookie cutters, Reindeer Food (small jars full of oatmeal and labeled "Reindeer Food"), Christmas books or coloring books. See Crafts for the following favor and prize ideas: Glitter Ball Ornaments, Salt Dough Ornaments, Paper Chains, Popcorn Garland, Reindeer Candy Canes, Beaded Candy Cane Ornaments, Beaded Ball Ornaments, Advent Tree, or Gingerbread Houses.

Kwanzaa Party

• *December 26–January 1* •

Kwanzaa is a seven-day African-American holiday remembering African American ancestors. The holiday is based on African harvest celebrations. It was founded in 1966 by Dr. Maulana "Ron" Karenga to celebrate the values of traditional African customs, and to teach African-Americans the history of their culture. The word Kwanzaa means "First Fruits" in Swahili. In Africa, harvest festivals are a part of everyday life. People celebrate the harvest with art, music and song. Dances are performed by masked dancers at an important time of the growing season. Simple gifts are exchanged during the celebration, known as zawadi. These gifts are often hand-crafted items, such as African-styled necklaces or jewelry that can be worn with African clothing.

Each family has its own way of celebrating Kwanzaa, but most follow the basic ideas or principles of Kwanzaa developed by Dr. Karenga. Kwanzaa isn't a religious holiday or an alternative to Christmas. It is a time for observing the seven principles of Kwanzaa, known as the nguzo saba developed by Dr. Karenga. On each of the seven days of this holiday, a candle is lit in the Kinara in observance of the seven principles.

INVITATIONS

Use a computer to print invitations with an African-print background, or use construction paper to make invitations that look like the African-American flag shown in the flag illustration (fig. 45).

DECORATIONS

• Hang an African-American flag, or bendera, in the party area. The colors

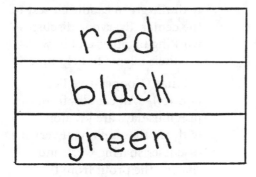

Fig. 45. African-American Flag

on the flag stand for the following: Red — for the blood of the African people; Black — for the color of the people; Green — for hope and the land of Africa. See Illustration (fig. 45).

- Place a hand-woven mat called a mkeka on a table.

- Place a kinara, or a seven-branched candelabra on the table. The kinara has seven candles placed in it called mishumaa saba. Three red candles stand on the left, three green on the right, and one black candle in the center.

- Place a bowl of fruits and vegetables on the table. Place dried ears of corn directly on the table mat or mkeka. One ear of corn should be placed on the mat for each child in the family. If there are no children, then place one ear of corn on the table. The corn symbolizes the importance of children for the future and success of the family.

- Place a unity cup called kikombe cha umoja on the mat. Everyone taking part in the celebration drinks from this cup as a symbol of unity in the family and community.

- The last items set on the mat are the gifts, or zawadi. The gifts may be hand-made items, poems, stories or a picture that the children have drawn for others. Basically, the gifts can be anything that is desired. It isn't necessary for it to be of a dollar value. It should come from the heart. These gifts are presented on the sixth day of Kwanzaa.

- Music — The music can be of anything that your family and guests enjoy hearing, or you can play spirited African drum selections.

🎉 FOOD 🎉

Serve traditional African or African-American dishes.

- Ham
- Catfish
- 2 or more of the following vegetables: yams, corn, okra, salad greens, collard greens, black-eyed peas, beans, or red beans and rice
- Cornbread or hushpuppies

The Traditional New Year's Day Menu:

- Black-eyed Peas — represent good luck or good fortune
- Fish — represent motivation and the desire to increase one's wealth
- Rice — represents prosperity
- Greens — represent money.

African-American Flag Cake

Make a cake that looks like the African-American flag. Use a 9 × 13-

inch baked cake. Frost the top third of the cake red. Frost the middle third with chocolate frosting. Frost the bottom third with green frosting. See flag illustration (fig. 45).

⛄ ARRIVAL ⛄ OF GUESTS

After the guests arrive, or just before the meal is to be served, light the candles on the kinara in observance of one of the seven principles on the corresponding day as follows:

1. Umoja (Unity) — The black candle is lit on the first day, the 26th of December. The person lighting the candle must talk about the importance of family, friends and neighbors. The unity cup is filled with juice or water by the person who lit the candle. He lifts the cup up high and shouts, "Harambee!" which means "Let's work together as a family and community." Everyone then says "Harambee!" seven times. Then each person takes a sip from the cup.

2. Kujicha (Self-Determination) — Re-light black candle and light red candle closest to center. Everyone discusses what they are doing or want to do for themselves and for others. Again, all drink from the unity cup.

3. Ujima (Collective Work & Responsibility) — All candles from the previous days are lit, along with the green candle closest to the center. Everyone discusses working together and how to use their talents to help others.

4. Ujamaa (Cooperative Economics) — All candles from the previous days are lit, along with another red one. Everyone discusses sharing work and sharing the profit from that work as a family and community.

5. Nia (Purpose) — All candles from the previous days are lit, along with a another green candle.

6. Kuumba (Creativity) — This day is celebrated on New Year's Eve — a great time to gather your friends and family. The first five candles are re-lit, along with a red candle. A feast is served and all discuss how they bring creativity into their homes, neighborhoods and communities. Crafts are made and music is played on this day. Afterward, the gifts are exchanged.

7. Imani (Faith) — This day is celebrated on New Year's Day, usually after the stroke of midnight. Now all of the candles are burning. Everyone again drinks from the unity cup and shouts one last "Harambee!"

🎉 CRAFTS 🎉

African Animal Masks

The Guro people of Côte d' Ivoire on the west coast of Africa make masks and costumes from wood and palm leaves. These masks are worn by dancers at ceremonies honoring people who have died. The animal masks may be of monkeys, antelopes, hyenas, dogs, hippopotami, elephants, etc. Have the children make these masks as described below. Play some spirited African drum selections and tell the children to perform a dance for you.

You will need:

Squares of posterboard, 1 per child
Pencils, 1 per child
Scissors
Felt-tip markers

What to do:

1. Give each child a square of cardboard and a pencil. Have them draw the outline of the type of animal that they would like on their mask, or pre-draw these for them before the party in different animal shapes. See illustration for an example of an African Animal Mask (fig. 46).

2. Have the children cut out the animal shapes.

3. Let them draw designs on the masks with the felt-tip markers.

4. Turn on the music! The children are now ready to have a dance with their masks!

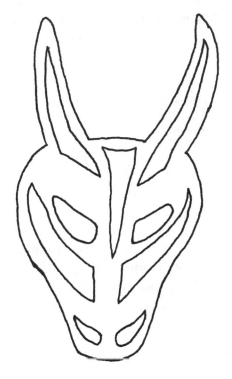

Fig. 46. African Animal Mask

Story Pictures

The Fon people of Benin (beh-NEEN) from the southern part of Africa tell their legends with brightly colored cloth pictures with shapes of people, ships, lions, wild hogs, leopards, fish, herons, etc. These shapes are cut from cotton cloth and sewn (or appliquéd) to a larger piece of contrasting fabric. The contrasting fabric usually being black or white.

If you will be making this craft with very young children, you may choose the following method to make the story pictures. But if the children are older, then you could choose, instead, to allow them to sew their story pictures.

You will need:

Large squares of black or white cloth, 1 per guest

Scraps of material in bright colors
Felt-tip markers, 1 per guest
Scissors, 1 per guest
Glue
Newspaper or a paper tablecloth

What to do:

1. Give each person a square of cloth, a pair of scissors, and a felt-tip marker.

2. Place all of the scrap material out onto a work area protected with newspaper or a paper tablecloth.

3. Tell the children to use different colors of material to draw shapes on. The shapes should be about things that are important to them such as a family pet, a bike, a relative, etc. Tell them to cut out the shapes.

4. Allow them to glue the shapes onto the square of cloth.

Painted Shirts

The Senufo (she-NOO-foh) people from the northern part of Côte d' Ivoire on the west coast of Africa make mud paintings on fabric. They collect river mud from nearby swamps to use as a kind of paint. When the mud is spread on the fabric in design patterns it stains the fabric in a deep black color. The designs are usually of animals that the Senufo hunt. It is believed that the spirits of the animals protect the hunters from danger and help bring a successful hunt. The designs serve another purpose — they camouflage the hunter.

Since you probably do not have access to deep black mud, you may choose to make your shirt as described below.

You will need:

T-shirts, 1 per guest
Black felt-tip markers
Black fabric paint
Disposable bowl
Paintbrushes, 1 per guest
Newspaper
Squares of cardboard, 1 per guest

What to do:

1. Cover the work area well with the newspaper to protect it from spills, and place a bowl of paint on top.

2. Place one square of cardboard inside of each shirt to keep the felt-tip marker and paint from bleeding through to the back of the shirt.

3. Use the black felt-tip marker to draw a design on the shirt. The designs can be of monkeys, crocodiles, turtles, or chameleons. An adult may want to draw the designs, as done by the Senufo, and the children may fill in the designs with paint — like coloring in a coloring book.

4. Set the shirts in a safe place and allow the paint to dry.

Beaded Jewelry

The Ndbele women of South Africa and Zimbabwe are known for their beautifully crafted jewelry. Supply the children with several bowls of different colored beads and some string. Have them make necklaces or bracelets with these beads.

🎉 GAMES AND 🎉 ACTIVITIES

Hire an Entertainer

Hire an African dance teacher or performer to come and show your guests some great dance steps. If you aren't able to find a professional in the field, check with your local cultural center, art commission or colleges for help. Play some African drum selections and get moving!

You could even hire someone who specializes in African village storytelling. Some play a host of African musical instruments, each with a unique sound.

Mancala

Purchase a Mancala game, found at many toy stores, and play it. A game very similar to Mancala is played all over the African continent.

Cattle Stockade

This circle game is played by children in Botswana, where cattle are an important part of their lives.

What to do:

1. The players all form a circle and join hands.

2. Two children are chosen to be

the "cattle" and stand in the center of the circle.

3. The children standing in the circle begin moving around, while the two cattle try to escape the inner circle by running under the other players' arms. The circle must not be broken.

4. If the cattle escape, they then join the circle, and two new players go into the center. You can choose different children to go into the center for each round. Or, you may choose to have the two children that were joined at the hands, where the circle was broken, go into the center. Continue playing for as long as you like or until everyone has had a turn in the center of the circle.

Dosu

This game is played by young girls in Benin, West Africa.

You will need:

Sand
Small objects (e.g., a rock or a toy)

What to do:

1. Before the party, create one small pile of sand for each player and hide one object in each pile.

2. During the party, have everyone choose a pile of sand and tell them to sit in front of it.

3. On the signal to go, all begin digging in their pile of sand for

the hidden object. The first one to find his hidden object is the winner. The winner may win a prize, but all get to keep the object hidden in their sand piles (if it is a toy).

Leopard Trap

In Sudan, children play this game which is much like London Bridge.

What to do:

1. Two players join their hands and raise them, creating a trap.

2. The other players form a line and dance as they pass through the trap — or under the two children's arms. As they do this, they chant the following rhyme:

> "Lion and leopard
> Lion and leopard
> Two night hunters
> Lion and leopard
> Lion and leopard
> Hunt their prey."

3. As the last word, "prey" is said the trap falls. The player to be caught is out of the game.

4. After two players are caught, a second trap is made behind the first with the two players who were caught. The game continues in this manner until there are only two players left.

The Cakewalk

Dance competitions are held all over Africa. Dance is considered a force that reveals a person's character and birthright among the Ngoni of Malawi.

This version of the game Cakewalk is different than the traditional Cakewalk game that is played in the circle formation to music. This version is a competition that was played by African slaves in Virginia at harvest time. The slaves danced along a path with pails of water on their heads. The object of the game was to see who could spill the least amount of water while remaining upright. The prize given to the winner was a cake.

Since Kwanzaa falls during the wintertime, and in most parts of the country it will be cold out, play this game indoors with empty cups. Put on some lively music and let the game begin! The player who first drops his cup loses. Award a cake to the winner.

⚐ FAVOR AND ⚐ PRIZE IDEAS

Items with the Kwanzaa theme or African designs on them (e.g., stickers, lapel pins, jewelry, pencils, erasers, pads of paper, etc.), cassettes of African music, inexpensive books on Africa or African culture, Painted Shirts (see Crafts), Story Pictures (see Crafts), African Animal Masks (see Crafts), or Beaded Jewelry (see Crafts).

Other Important Days and Holidays

Super Bowl Sunday

This falls on one Sunday in January (usually two weeks after the play-offs)

Ask guests to come dressed in T-shirts or sweatshirts in team colors. Assign seating sections for opposing teams. The host or hostess could wear a whistle around his or her neck. Decorate the table to look like a playing field by using a green plastic or paper tablecloth with white yard lines on it. Use white tape or white crepe paper to create the yard lines. For a centerpiece, use pennants, pompoms, footballs or megaphones. Serve simple to prepare foods such as jambalaya, chili, sandwiches, hot dogs, chicken wings, etc. Place snack foods, such as peanuts, popcorn, and chips, on the coffee table. Give away inexpensive football souvenirs as party favors such as pennants, cups, posters, football cards, etc.

April Fool's Day

April 1st

April Fool's Day is a day of practical jokes and silly pranks. Start the day off on the right note by fooling someone.

Earth Day

April 22nd

Have a community cleanup on Earth Day. Look around your neighborhood, church or school, or even place of business and you are sure to find unsightly trash somewhere. Ask for volunteers to pitch in and help pick up the litter. Ask the volunteers to also bring cans or bundles of newspapers on cleanup day. You can bring them to a recycling center and turn them in for money to use for your organization. Use the money to plant flowers or trees. If your community or your child's school does not have a recycling program, start one. Use recycled materials to make craft projects on Earth Day. One good craft idea for children would be to use cleaned-out frozen juice containers or vegetable cans as pencil holders. Cover and decorate the containers or cans by gluing on old wallpaper scraps.

National Teacher Appreciation Week

First week of May

Have your child show his teachers how much he appreciates them by making a homemade card and bringing them a small gift during this week. Some gift ideas are an apple, a flower, a plant, a box of candy, stationery, stickers for school papers, etc. During this week, many schools choose to do one thing special for the teachers every day of the week. Some ideas are: give a basket of goodies; secretly send a note home to each parent in the school asking them to have the children write the teacher a note saying why they appreciate their teacher; purchase or make a card for all of the children to sign; treat them to lunch and have a volunteer come and watch the class, etc.

Mother's Day

Second Sunday in May

If you are a mother reading this, you may need to give the following hints to your husband to pass on to your children. Sometimes a little reminder is needed to get results. I actually had to write a note to my husband one year reminding him about Mother's Day. Ask for the day's meals to be made for you. Restaurants may be extremely busy on Mother's Day. So, a quiet day at home might be your thing. Resist the urge to help in the kitchen. Kick back and enjoy the show. Plan on playing board games or outdoor games with your family. The name of the game is to "relax" on this day set aside especially for you.

If your children have no money (and you would rather have help around the house, than a gift), hint to your husband that you would like for them to make you a coupon book with redemptions. He can ask your children to secretly make the book for you before Mother's Day. The following are some ideas that they can use:

> One car wash
> One back rub
> One whole-house cleaning
> One dinner made by me
> One dish washing
> One foot massage
> One entire basement/garage
>   cleaning

End your day with a nice quiet, relaxing bath!

Memorial Day

Last Monday in May

Memorial day is a day to remember those of our ancestors and family members who we have lost, and to remember the soldiers who have died defending our country. In honor of those that have died, flags are flown at half-mast. Military and civic parades take place in many cities across the nation. Families bring flowers to the graves of their loved ones. You may want to offer to bring an elderly relative or friend to the cemetery with you to visit someone who has passed on. If they are unable to drive anymore or getting out alone is difficult, having you to assist them should really be appreciated. Perhaps you could offer to stop by the florist to help them pick out a bouquet of flowers, or maybe even take them out to breakfast or lunch. Afterwards, go back to their home and go through photo albums together.

Father's Day

Third Sunday in June

If you are a father reading this, pass these hints on to your family. Tell your wife to pass the hints on to your children. As with Mother's Day on page 182, tell your wife to have your children make you a coupon book of redemptions. Sometimes your child's time can be more valuable to you than a gift, and many children just don't have a lot of money to spend. The following are some ideas to have your children use:

One back massage
One foot massage
Trip to your favorite restaurant
Day trip to a place of his choice
One grass cutting
One yard cleaning
One car wash
One garage cleaning

Some gift ideas are belts, wallets, neckties, slippers, money clips, socks, underwear, shirts, briefcase, nice pens, tools, golf balls, etc.

Today is Dad's day to relax! He should be able to kick up his feet and do absolutely nothing. If you have a hammock, send him to it for a quiet, undisturbed nap. If he enjoys reading, give him his favorite reading material,

a glass of his favorite drink, and leave him alone to read.

First Day of Summer

June 21st

Celebrate by playing in the sprinkler or pool. Have water gun fights.

Labor Day

First Monday in September

Labor Day is a holiday in honor of working people. It is a day to take a rest from your work. Have a picnic or a barbecue with family and friends. See Fourth of July Party for some fun game ideas to play.

United Nations Day

October 24th

Celebrate with games, crafts and food from around the world. Order food from local ethnic restaurants. Some restaurants will be willing to donate the food for school activities, as long as you are reasonable with your request and you offer them free advertisement in your school newsletter for their donation. Basically, give them a good plug in the newsletter for helping out your school. Send the restaurants a copy of your school newsletter, so that they know how much you appreciate what they have done for your school. Ask guests to come dressed in a costume from the country of their choice. Award prizes for the best costume. Play ethnic music from around the world. Invite a visitor from another country to come and tell about their homeland. Perhaps the visitor could tell a story, play an instrument, show the children a few dance steps, or teach a craft. Use maps, flags, dolls, clothing and other items from around the world for decorations. Use a world globe as a table centerpiece. Give coins, stamps, and travel brochures from other countries as party favors.

Games for Any Occasion

The games in this chapter are games that can be played at any type of holiday, birthday or school party. Many of them are perfect for school carnivals, church carnivals, neighborhood block parties, children's festivals or other events.

How to Make Bean Bags for Tossing Games

You will need:

Two 5 × 5-inch pieces of fabric
Needle and thread, or a sewing machine
Scissors
Dried beans, rice, or popping corn

What to do:

1. Sew the two squares of fabric together on three sides, with the fabric designs facing together.

2. Turn the sewn sides in.

3. Fill the pouches with dried beans, rice or popping corn.

4. Sew the open end closed.

Games to Play with Beanbags

• Draw a target on the pavement with chalk or tape. Let the children toss the beanbags and try to hit the targets. Each target could have a score or a picture. The highest score wins or anyone hitting the correct picture wins.

• Cut the bottoms off of plastic milk jugs to use like scoops. Let the children try to catch the beanbags with the scoops.

Balloon Prize

You will need:

Balloons and small prizes

What to do:

1. Before the party, stick small objects inside of balloons, inflate and tie them closed.
2. Attach the balloons to a fence, cardboard, plywood, a tree, corkboard, etc.
3. During the party, one at a time, allow the children to select a balloon.
4. Pop the balloon with a pin to reveal their prize.

Variation: You could also put a piece of paper in each balloon with the name of the prize on the paper.

Bottle Cap Target

You will need:

A hula hoop, string, or chalk
10 "metal" bottle caps (plastic caps tend to bounce out of the circle)
Bowl

What to do:

1. Make a circle target on the floor using the hula hoop, string, or chalk.
2. Have the children stand behind a marked line 5–8 feet from the circle.
3. Allow the children to take turns tossing a bowl full of the 10 metal bottle caps into the circle. Award a piece of candy for each cap that goes into the circle, or if they get 5 in, award a prize.

Penny Drop

You will need:

Large round fishbowl or other similar round bowl full of water
Small clear drinking glass or a small clear glass jar
5 bright pennies
Pencil and paper to keep score, optional

What to do:

1. Sink the drinking glass or jar in the center of the large bowl and set it on the bottom.
2. Have the children take turns trying to drop the pennies, one at a time, into the small glass.
3. If playing at a carnival, anyone getting 2 pennies into the small jar wins a prize. If playing at a holiday or birthday party, write down each child's score after his turn. The winner gets to keep all of the pennies outside of the small glass, or give him a prize. The child who comes in second place gets to keep all of the pennies inside of the jar, or give him a smaller prize.

Floating Blocks

You will need:

10–20 wooden blocks with different colors painted on only one side
Small child's pool or tub of water

What to do:

1. Float the wooden blocks in the pool or tub of water.
2. Allow each child a turn to pick

one block. The color on the block chosen determines the prize won. Green might win a ball, red might win a ring, etc.

Caution: Do not leave children unattended around the tub or pool of water. Take the tub or pool of water away from the party area after using and dump the water out.

Bucket Toss

You will need:

3–4 buckets, each labeled with a number
3 balls or beanbags

What to do:

1. Line up the buckets, one behind the other, number 1 being the first bucket, number 2 being the second bucket and so on.

2. Stand the children behind a marked line 5–8 feet away from the first bucket.

3. Allow each child to toss the 3 balls or beanbags. The bucket that the child gets a ball or beanbag into determines their prize. The first bucket would be a tiny prize, the second a medium prize and the last bucket would be a prize of more value.

Clothespin Drop

You will need:

Large wide mouth jar, such as a mayonnaise jar
Chair
Pencil and paper for keeping score

What to do:

1. Place the jar on the floor. Next to the jar, place a chair, with the back of the chair facing the bottle.

2. Have the children take turns dropping 10 clothespins into the bottle, from the back of the chair. Watch for cheaters! The elbows must stay at the top of the chair. Write down each child's score after his turn. The child to get the most clothespins into the bottle wins.

Variation: Place the bottle below a porch or deck. A distance of about 3–5 feet below would be good. Let the children drop the clothespins into the bottle from the top of the porch, while keeping their elbows on the railing. Be sure that there is a railing and that it is secure to prevent anyone from falling. The child to get the most clothespins into the bottle wins.

Bubble Gum Blowing Contest

Pass out large pieces of bubble gum and see who can blow the biggest bubble.

Broom Relay

You will need:

2 brooms
Inflated balloons, 1 per player

What to do:

1. Divide the children into two equal teams and give each player an inflated balloon. Have

some extras on hand in case some pop. Stand the players behind a marked starting line.

2. Hand the first child in each line a broom.

3. Set a laundry basket or a box about 15–20 feet away from the start line.

4. On the signal to go, the first child on each team must sweep the balloon with his broom into laundry basket or box.

5. He then runs back to his team and hands the broom to the next teammate in line. He does the same as the first child in line. The game continues in this manner until a team has all of its members complete the task. They are declared the winning team.

Goose Egg

You will need:

Egg shaped pieces of white cardboard, 1 per player

What to do:

1. Before the party, write "GOOSE" on only one of the eggs.

2. During the party, seat all of the children in a circle on the floor or around a table.

3. Pass out one cardboard egg to each child, making sure that the word "GOOSE" is pointing down.

4. At a signal to go, each child passes their egg in a clockwise direction by sliding it along on the floor or table, and they keep passing the eggs from one player to the next.

5. At the signal to stop, they all turn their eggs over, and whoever has the "GOOSE" egg is out of the game.

6. Remove one of the ordinary eggs after each child is out, shuffle the others, and re-distribute them. The game goes on until only one child is left. He is the winner.

Variation: If desired, use holiday shapes instead of the egg shape.

Hide the Object

Hide one object that fits the party theme, such as a stuffed bunny for the Easter Party. Explain to the children that when they get close to the object you will say "warm" and if they are far away you will say "cold". Let them all search together as a group or separately. If playing it as a group, award all a prize when the object is found. If playing it singly, award the child to find the object a prize.

Dart Gun Game

Set up several lightweight objects on a table or a porch railing. A good example would be to use toy soldiers for the Fourth of July Party. Let the children take turns shooting at the objects. Give the children 3 shots each. The child to knock the most down wins a prize, or any child to knock 2 down wins a prize.

Candy Scramble

You will need:

Plenty pieces of wrapped candy
Bags labeled with the children's
names

What to do:

1. This is much like trying to get
   the fallen candy from a piñata,
   only there is no piñata. Spread
   some wrapped candy on the
   floor or ground.

2. Pass out one bag to each child.

3. Have the children form a circle
   around the candy and get down
   on all fours.

4. At the signal to go, all crawl to
   the candy and try to get as
   much as they can.

Balloon Volleyball

Inflate a balloon and tell the children that the goal is to hit it back and forth to one another without letting it fall to the ground. The children may use their hands or heads to hit the balloon and try to keep it in the air. If you like, use a rope or string to divide the team sides. Any time a team lets the balloon drop to the ground a score is given to the other team. The first team to reach a score of 15 wins.

Jacks

The game of Jacks has been played by children all over the world for many centuries.

You will need:

Small rubber ball

6–12 six-pointed jacks (if you don't
have jacks, use small stones, seeds
or twigs)

What to do:

1. The player throws the jacks
   onto the ground or floor in
   front of him.

2. Using the same hand, he
   throws the ball up into the
   air and picks up 1 jack after
   the ball has bounced. He
   catches the ball with the same
   hand.

3. Next he picks up 2 jacks at a
   time, then 3, and so on until he
   has picked up 6 or 12 at one
   time. The first player to complete all steps without missing
   any jacks is the winner.

Park It

You will need:

Cardboard box
Scissors or a craft knife
Felt-tip marker
5 marbles
Pencil and paper for keeping score

What to do:

1. Before the party, cut five openings in the bottom of a cardboard box. Make some openings larger than others. Give the larger openings a lower score and give the smaller openings a higher score, by writing a number above the opening.

2. During the party, let the children take turns trying to shoot 5 marbles into the "garage door

openings" to try and "park" the marbles.

3. After each child has a turn, write his score down. The child with the highest score wins. An appropriate prize would be a small toy car. For a carnival, you could give a prize according to the hole that the marble goes in. Anyone shooting a marble into a small hole could win a nice prize.

Muffin Tin Toss

You will need:

Muffin tins
Paper
Felt-tip markers
3 Ping-Pong balls
Pencil and paper for keeping score

What to do:

1. Line 2 or more muffin tins side by side on the floor.

2. Place pieces of paper that have numbers written on them inside of the muffin cups.

3. Have the children toss the 3 ping-pong balls into the muffin tins. The numbers on the cups each count as a point. Add up the numbers after each child takes a turn. The child with the highest score wins a prize.

Variation: When playing this game at a carnival, use a lot of old muffin tins. Paint some cups different colors. Anyone to get a ping-pong ball into a colored cup wins a prize. The amount of balls that fall into the colored cups determines the prize.

Variation: Play this game with wrapped candy. The child to get the most candy in the tins wins all of the candy that has been thrown into the tins.

Candy Toss

You will need:

Large paper grocery bags or plastic containers to fit the theme, 1 per child
Felt-tip markers or paint
Wrapped candy
String or masking tape

What to do:

1. Draw or paint designs and guests names on their bag or container before the day of the party, but only on one side. Or, you could allow guests to decorate these themselves as they arrive. Allow them to dry.

2. Stand the bags side by side with the decorated side hidden from view.

3. Give each child an equal amount of candy and stand them behind a throwing line marked with string or tape. The children are to toss the candy into the bags without knowing which bags is their bag.

4. When all have tossed their candy, have the children come around to the other side of the bags to see who got the most candy.

Hold Your Breath

You will need:

Empty soda bottles, 1 per player
Toothpicks, 20 per player

What to do:

1. Seat all of the children in a circle on the floor or around a table.

2. Pass out one soda bottle and 20 toothpicks to each player.

3. On the signal to go, all try to place their toothpicks on top of the mouth of the bottle crosswise. The first child to get all of his toothpicks to stay on top of the bottle is the winner.

Variation: Place only one soda bottle on the floor or table. Have each child take a turn at putting a toothpick across the mouth if the bottle. If a player knocks any off, he must then keep what he has knocked off. The first player to use up all of his toothpicks is the winner.

The Door Keeper

You will need:

A ball

What to do:

1. Have all of the children stand in a circle with their legs apart and their feet touching the next child's feet.

2. Choose one child to go into the center of the circle and hand him a ball. Use an ordinary size ball for young children and use a smaller ball for older children.

3. The child in the center of the circle must try to roll the ball through the legs of the other children, who try to stop the ball by closing their legs.

4. A player is out when the ball makes it between his legs. When everyone is out, the game starts over again with a new child in the center of the circle.

Variation: If you like, send the first child to have the ball go through his legs go into the center of the circle and switch places with the child in the center.

String Hunt

You will need:

Yarn cut into various lengths, anywhere from 2 inches to 2 feet

What to do:

1. Hide the strings around the house or yard.

2. At the signal to go, everyone races to find the strings.

3. After all of the strings have been found, everyone gathers around and places their strings, end to end, along the floor or ground. The child with the longest piece of string and the child with the most strings win a prize.

Give It Up

You will need:

A container such as a hat, basket, or bucket that fits the party theme

Wrapped candies, 1 piece per child
Decorated cardboard holiday shape
Holiday music or music that fits the
theme

What to do:

1. Seat all of the children in a circle on the floor or ground.

2. Place the hat, basket or bucket the center of the circle. Some container examples to use are: a Leprechaun hat for a St. Patrick's party, an Easter basket for an Easter party, a plastic Halloween pumpkin for a Halloween party, etc.

3. Hand each child a wrapped piece of candy that fits the theme.

4. Hand a shape that fits the theme to one child in the circle. Some ideas to use are: a painted cardboard rainbow for a St. Patrick's party, an Easter bunny for Easter, a witch for Halloween.

5. At the start of the music, the shape gets passed around the circle in a clockwise direction. When the music stops, the child holding the shape must place his piece of candy in the hat, basket or bucket in the center of the circle.

6. The music begins again and the game continues as before. The last child still left with his piece of candy wins the entire container full of candy.

Tin Can Throw

You will need:

6 aluminum cans
3 tennis balls

What to do:

1. Set up a stack of aluminum cans, putting several on the bottom and one less can for every layer on top of the next.

2. Stand each child 10 feet away and give them three shots with tennis balls. See how many cans he can knock down. Make sure that there isn't anyone or any pets behind the cans. Write down each child's score after his turn. The child who knocks the most cans down wins a prize.

Handkerchief Catch

You will need:

Handkerchief or bandanna

What to do:

1. Have all of the children stand in a circle and choose one child to go in the center of the circle with the handkerchief or bandanna.

2. The child in the center throws the handkerchief or bandanna up in the air above him and calls out a player's name.

3. The child whose name is called must catch the handkerchief or bandanna before it falls to the ground. If he does not catch it, he becomes the next child in

the center of the circle. If he does catch it, the child in the center remains in the center and the game proceeds as before. Play the game until everyone has had a turn in the center or play for about 10 minutes.

What's in the Bag?

You will need:

10 lunch bags, each numbered

Items to go in each bag (e.g., a stuffed animal, a bottle of glue, a golf ball, a sponge, etc.)

Stapler

Piece of paper number 1–10, 1 per player

Pencils, 1 per player

What to do:

1. Before the party, place one item in each bag. Use objects that are tricky to determine for older children. Staple the bags closed, so that no one can peek inside of them.

2. Place the bags all along a table or around the room.

3. Give each child a numbered piece of paper and a pencil to write down what they guess is in each bag. The children may pick up the bags and feel them to try and determine what is in the bag, but they cannot peek inside of the bag. Give the children about 10–15 minutes to write their answers down. The child to guess the most correct wins.

Heads Up 7-Up

This is a game that will require 20 or more guests to play.

1. Choose 7 children to go to the other end of the room. The rest of the children must cover their eyes or put their head on a desk or a table.

2. The children covering their eyes or laying their heads down must hold up one of their thumbs. The 7 children at the front of the room must each touch only one person on the thumb. As soon as a child is touched on the thumb, he puts his thumb in his fist, so that others will know that he has been touched.

3. When the 7 children have finished they all meet back at the other end of the room, and the adult tells everyone to uncover their eyes.

4. Anyone who was touched on the thumb must stand up. Give each child one turn to guess who touched their thumb. If they guess correctly, the person who touched them must sit down and the child who guessed correctly takes his place for the next round. Any of the 7 players who is not figured out, gets to be one of the "7-Up" again for the next round.

Silverware Tic-Tac-Toe

If you will be holding your party in a restaurant, here is game to keep the children busy while waiting on their food.

You will need:

Forks and knives (4 of any combination)

Different colored sugar packets (usually found on restaurant tables)

What to do:

1. Use the forks and knives to make a 9-square grid on the tabletop.

2. Ask each player to choose a partner and sit next to or across from one another.

3. Hand one player 4 colored sugar packets of one color and hand the other player four colored sugar packets of another color for the markers.

4. Play just as you would ordinary tic-tac-toe. The object of the game is to get a straight line or row of 3 in your own color. The rows may be either vertically, horizontally or diagonally. Each player takes one turn at a time, placing one of his sugar packets in a square on the grid until someone wins, or the board is covered. If no one

wins, that is called "cats", the grid is cleared and the game is played again, until someone wins, or until the waitress comes with the food.

Backward Race

You will need:

2 long pieces of string or garden hoses

What to do:

1. Have all of the children choose one partner.

2. Mark a line on the ground with the string or garden hose.

3. Mark another line about 20–30 feet away.

4. Have all of the players stand behind one line and stand back to back with their partners. They are to interlock arms at the elbow.

5. At the signal to go, the interlocked partners race to the goal. One of the partners runs forward to the goal line and the other partner will run forward on the way back to the start line. The fastest couple to return to the start line wins.

Holiday Piñatas

What would a holiday party be without a piñata (peen-YA-tah) filled with yummy goodies and prizes? Children absolutely love them! Piñatas have been adding excitement to parties for over 400 years. The origin of the piñata is not known, but some historians believe that it may have come from China or Italy. Piñatas were traditionally used to celebrate a good harvest and were filled with fruits and vegetables. Today they are mainly used to celebrate birthdays and holidays.

Holiday themed piñatas can be purchased at many toy stores, department stores and party supply stores, but if you cannot find one that fits your party theme, make your own following the instructions in this chapter. The piñata can serve as a decoration and a game activity during the party. But be forewarned that once you begin using piñatas at your celebrations, your guests will love them so much that they will come to expect them at future parties!

Papier-mâché Recipe and Piñata Base Directions

The following recipe should not be doubled or tripled. Since piñatas are made in several stages and the paste does not save well, make more paste as it is needed.

You will need:

Large bowl (preferably an old bowl)

Medium bowl (preferably an old bowl)

1 cup of flour

¾ cup warm water

Newspaper

Inflated balloon

Cardboard for added features: paper towel tubes, toilet paper tubes, notepad backing, etc.

Wire coat hanger

Duct tape

Piñata filler: trinkets, soft well-wrapped candy, unshelled peanuts, filled lunch bags, etc.

What to do:

1. Tear the newspaper into strips along the edge of a countertop or a squared surface. The strips should be about 1 inch wide by 5 or 6 inches long. Try to use newspaper from the classified section, since it has less color printing in it. The color can show through if you will be using tissue paper to cover the piñata. Do not cut the newspaper with scissors, because the rough edges caused from tearing actually adhere better than a very smooth cut. You may need to experiment a little with tearing it in different ways to get it to tear properly.

2. Place the inflated balloon inside of the large bowl to hold it in place as it is being worked on. This will become the base or body of your piñata.

3. Remove any rings from your hands to keep the flour mixture off of them. Pour the flour into the medium bowl. Add the warm water and stir. You can use a spoon to remove the lumps or you may squeeze the paste between your hands. Remove all of the lumps so that the paste is smooth and like ordinary white glue. The paste should not be thick like pudding.

4. Dip one strip of newspaper into the flour mixture at a time. Do not let the newspaper soak in the mixture for too long or it will become over-saturated and tear. To remove the excess paste, hold the newspaper strip up with one hand and gently squeeze off the excess paste with two fingers from your other hand.

5. Place one strip over the balloon at a time. The strips should not all be in the same direction. Put them on in a criss-cross fashion. Try not to place too many strips on top of on another, or it will take much longer for the layer to dry. Leave a space that is not covered with strips for a hole to put the goodies in the piñata. Check each individual piñata instruction in this chapter for the placement of the hole.

6. Dry completely between layers. It usually takes one entire day to completely dry. You can speed the drying process by placing the piñata outdoors on a warm day, but temperatures above 80° may cause the balloon to expand and pop.

7. Once the piñata is completely dry, you may add on additional layers following steps 1–6. Add 2–3 layers for small children and 4–6 for older children. The strength of the piñata will depend on the strength of the guests. Add on any facial features or body limbs to the piñata at this time. Use strips of papier-mâché (paper-ma-SHAY) to attach the features.

8. When all of the layers have dried, pop the balloon with a pin. The kids get a thrill out of watching what happens to the balloon, so you may want to

have them watch. Remove the popped balloon and discard it.

9. Bend the wire coat hanger to fit inside of the piñata as the piñata hanger. Form it so that it fit snugly next to the edges of the piñata. The hook of the coat hanger should be sticking out of the top of the piñata hole. Bend the hook into a hanging loop using a pair of pliers. Bend it so that no sharp points are sticking out. Cover any sharp points with duct tape.

10. Stuff the piñata with ¾ of the chosen piñata filler. Set some of the filler aside for anyone who does not get enough during the game. Seal the piñata shut by wrapping more strips of papier-mâché around the top of the coat hanger at the opening. Completely cover the opening of the piñata. If the shape needs to be more rounded to look realistic, add a ball of newspaper over the hole and then cover it with papier-mâché. You may want to apply several layers of papier-mâché over the opening to give the hanger added strength.

11. After the piñata has completely dried, decorate the piñata according to the instructions given in the following pages for each piñata, or make your own kind of piñata. A piñata can be covered by wrapping long strands of crepe paper around it, or you can even paint it. To make a fur-type piñata cover, take 2- to 3-inch-wide colored strips of tissue paper, fold them in half and cut slits at the unfolded edge. To attach, glue the strips to the piñata, working from the bottom of the piñata on up to the top. Construction paper can be used for features such as the eyes, mouth, belt buckles, etc. Yarn works great for mustaches and hair. Use a colored plastic disposable bowl for a hat. Basically, just let your imagination take over and get creative. After you have made one piñata, you will be amazed at how fun they are to make with your family. See Hanging and Breaking instructions in this chapter to learn how to play the game.

Variation: A strong rope may be used instead of the wire coat hanger as a piñata hanger. The rope may be wrapped around the outside of the piñata and held in place with papier-mâché layers. Another version is to tie a strong rope around a wooden dowel or an unsharpened pencil. Place the wooden dowel or pencil inside of the piñata and pull up on it. Then close the hole of the piñata by wrapping strips of papier-mâché around the dowel or pencil to secure it.

Bull or Ox Piñata

Follow the Piñata Base Directions as instructed, using one larger balloon for the body and one smaller one for the head. Attach the head to the body with strips of papier-mâché after it is complete. The hole left for the hanger and the candy will be on the side of the balloon. In step 7, use 4 toilet paper rolls or paper towel rolls to add on the legs. Cut a few ¾-inch slits on one end of each roll. Spread out the slit to make a base. This will help the legs stay on better. Attach the legs with one layer of papier-mâché strips, both inside of the "leg" and outside. Crumple two pieces of newspaper to form the bull or ox horns, and attach with a layer of papier-mâché. Once the piñata is completely dry, cover it with brown or red tissue paper strips that resemble fur (see step 11 of Piñata Base Directions). Use tan or black tissue paper to cover the horns and make hooves. Glue it in place. Use construction paper for the eyes. Draw the mouth on with a black felt-tip marker. Black yarn makes for a great tail when tied together. The best way to hold it in place is with hot glue. See illustration (fig. 47).

Fig. 47. Bull or Ox Piñata

Egg Piñata

Follow the Piñata Base Directions as instructed. This is probably one of the easiest piñatas that you can make since it only requires using a balloon. There are no limbs or facial features that must be added on. Once the piñata is completely done drying, wrap one or

more colors of crepe paper or tissue paper around the piñata and glue them in place. If desired, tape unique designs or pictures made out of construction paper to the piñata. See illustration (fig. 48).

Fig. 48. Egg Piñata

Mexican Amigo Piñata

Follow the Piñata Base Directions as instructed. In step 7, use a triangle shaped piece of cardboard that is bent in half for the nose. Attach the nose with a layer of papier-mâché. When the piñata is completely dry, paint the face a flesh color with acrylic paint. Paint on a mouth with red lips and white teeth. Color lines in between the teeth with black paint. For the eyes, paint on white ovals, with brown circles on them for the eye color, black pupils, and two tiny black lines at the outer corner of each eye for eyelashes. Paint on black hair and black ear shapes. Make a mustache by cutting black yarn and by laying several layers on top of one another. Tie at the center with another piece of yarn. Glue it on under the nose and slightly spread apart so that you can see the teeth. If desired, when the piñata is completely dry, place an old sombrero hat on the head by cutting a hole in the top, center of the hat and slipping the hat over the piñata hanger. Color a large sheet of paper with Mexican designs, using crayons or paint. Your child may enjoy doing this for you. The paper should appear as a Mexican serape. Attach the paper to a long wrapping paper tube with tape or glue. The ends of the wrapping paper tube should stick out a few inches on each side of the paper to appear as arms. Trace your child's hands (or a small child's hands) onto a piece of cardboard. Cut the hand shapes out and stick them into the ends of the wrapping paper tubes. Attach a piece of self-adhesive Velcro to the bottom of the head and another to the paper on the center of the "serape" (the end with the wrapping paper tube). Connect the serape to the head to appear as the body. You will now have a very lifelike and impressive piñata! See illustration (fig. 49).

Variation: You can make the sombrero hat out of a cut and shaped piece of heavyweight construction paper instead of using a real sombrero hat. This looks really good, but requires more work.

Hanging the Piñata

There a various ways that the piñata can be hung and where and how

Fig. 49. Mexican Amigo Piñata

you hang your piñata will all depend on your own individual circumstances and preferences. Always keep safety in mind when hanging the piñata. It should not be hung near light fixtures or breakables. If the piñata is filled with candy that can melt, then do not hang it in the direct sunlight. The pinata should be hung just before your guests will arrive, if it will be hung outdoors. Make sure that you hang the piñata to just above the head of your average guest's height. To determine this, you may need to use your child. Check to be sure that the area under and around the piñata is free from any objects that might hurt the children. Spread a large tarp underneath the piñata to keep the candy and prizes clean when they fall to the ground. The following are some ways that you can hang the piñata:

Variation 1: Hang the piñata from a very strong tree limb that extends out and well away from the tree trunk. Use a strong rope to hang the piñata from the tree branch.

Variation 2: If you don't have a strong tree branch, but do have two big trees, tie a rope between the two trees. Hang the piñata from the center of that rope with another rope. Some people like to use this method, but do not like to tie the rope to the center of the suspended rope. They instead just use a very long rope and toss it over the suspended rope. You can raise or lower the piñata to the necessary height by holding the rope at the opposite end of the piñata with this method. This works well at parties with children of different heights.

Variation 3: Hang the piñata from the joist in a garage or basement. Just be sure to hang the piñata within a safe swinging distance from any poles or other objects.

Variation 4: Hang the piñata from your garage door metal runners, if your metal runners are very strong and secure. Hang a long rope from the strongest point (usually the far top end near the brackets that support the runners). Hang the piñata from the center of the suspended rope.

Breaking the Piñata

As your guests arrive and see the piñata, they may become excited and attempt to swing at the piñata before it is time to play the game. So, you will have to keep a close eye on them and warn them not to touch it until it is time.

The type of piñata, the strength of the piñata, and your own preference will determine which item you will use to break you piñata. If you put too many layers on the piñata it will be difficult too break and may require a baseball bat to get it open. Some people prefer to use a cut broomstick handle, but I do not. I think that a broomstick handle can snap and fly off into the air causing a dangerous situation. Others prefer to use a piñata bat. Piñata bats work well with purchased piñatas.

You will need:

Blindfold (a bandanna or a scarf) and a clothespin to secure it

Baseball bat or a piñata bat (if it is sturdy)

Goody holders: plastic goody bags, paper bags, holiday buckets, baskets, etc.

What to do:

1. Label the goody holders with the children's names before the day of the party.

2. Line all of the children up, with the youngest or smallest children first, in a half circle around the piñata. It is very important to keep the bigger and stronger children at the end of the line, otherwise the piñata will be broken before anyone gets a turn to swing at it. Make sure that the children are always at a safe swinging distance throughout the entire game. Pass out the goody holders and make sure that you have your reserved filler handy.

3. Blindfold the first child in line and place his goody bag where he can easily get to it, or have an adult hold it for him and be ready to pass it to him if he should need it.

4. Gently turn the child around 3 times to throw off his sense of

direction. Hand him the baseball bat or piñata bat, and get
everyone, including yourself,
out of his way. Tell the child to
hit the piñata. Allow 2 swings
at the piñata. Cheer on the person up to bat so that he will
feel good. If the children are
real young, you might want to
give them extra swings. If you
have a really large group of
children, you might choose to
only allow one swing at the
piñata so that everyone gets a
turn.

5. If the child breaks the piñata,
and the goodies fall out, then
let all of the children scramble
for the candy. Take the bat
away from the hitter so that he
doesn't accidentally hit someone. Help the child up to bat
get the blindfold off quickly
and hand him his goody
holder. If he doesn't break the
piñata, then the next child in
line gets turn. This continues
until someone breaks the
piñata. Sometime only a few

pieces of candy will fall
through a small break. If this
happens, you may want to tell
the children to wait until all of
the candy has fallen. Continue
playing until it fully bursts
open. As the children are
scrambling for the candy, check
inside of the piñata, sometimes
more candy will be left inside.
Throw this candy onto the
ground with the others, or give
it to a child who hasn't gotten
enough along with your reserved candy. Make sure that
everyone receives some candy
to prevent any hurt feelings.

6. After all of the goodies have
been gathered, have the children help you pick up all of the
broken piñata pieces and discard them in the trash. Also remove the hanging remains of
the piñata and discard it. The
children will attempt to continue swinging at it if you
don't. Put the bat away so that
the children won't be tempted
to swing it.

Index